May the Real Paul Come Forth

Who Is Paul?

By Isaac Levy

PRESS

May the Real Paul Come Forth
Who Is Paul?
by Isaac Levy

Printed in the United States of America

ISBN 9781624190131

All Scripture is taken from the Torah Prophets and writings New Testament Version

All Old Testament Scripture references, unless otherwise noted, are from the author's own translation/transliteration from the Hebrew Tanach.

The author added all boldface emphases and text within brackets in Scripture passages.

> NIV: New International Version
> KJV: King James Version
> ASV: American Standard Version
> NASB: New American Standard Bible

The comments in this book are given from a Hebrew point of view, thus the names mentioned are addressed in the original Hebrew.

www.xulonpress.com

ACKNOWLEDGMENTS

*T*o Mark Kelldorf, who has supported and encouraged me for years by telling me how much this type of study book is needed by the general audience. This book is for people who do not speak the Hebrew language, nor have any idea how the Jewish people study the Torah and their cultural distinctives.

To Sandi, my wife, who insisted I take my time and deliver a book that makes sense, is easy to read and easy to study.

To my children Daliah, Daniela and Natan, who kept pushing me to stay the course and not give up.

To my family of Beit Or: John Cavendar, Bob Cheney, Dr. Ron Weaks, Jeremy Barnes, and Jesse Markovits for their prayers and encouragement to complete the book; to Joyce Tapia and Sharyl Markovits who were always eager to help me with grammar; to Bobby Jensen and Sal Abate for motivating me to share the truth about Shaul (Paul) on YouTube and for their help with a cover design for the book; To Toni Ogle for helping me the most with editing.

FOREWORD

I have had the honor and privilege of knowing Rabbi Isaac Levy for more than twenty-five years. Isaac has been and continues to be a teacher, counselor, mentor and my trusted friend.

This book, written for the glory of God, is yet another example of Isaac teaching God's Word through revelation. The goal is for us all to develop a deeper understanding of the Holy Scripture.

The desire and passion to reveal the truth of God's Word is evident throughout this book. Isaac's use of such God-given tools such as knowing the Hebrew language, understanding and living the customs of the Bible, properly using Hebrew idioms and teaching how to truly study the Bible makes this book beyond a unique adventure.

The enlightenment begins when we understand that there are no contradictions in the Bible and that God, like His law, is complete and never changing.

As the light shines deep in our soul, all our prayers and goals should be:

> *That through the Holy Scriptures, the man of God may be thoroughly furnished unto our good works (**2 Timothy 3:17**).*

Mark S. Kelldorf,
Believer, friend, scientist

Seat of Moshe from the Synagogue of Chorazin

*A*rcheologist found this unique treasure in the synagogue in the city of Chorazin, which is nine hundred feet above the Sea of Galilee. Chorazin was one of numerous towns that thrived in Galilee after the destruction of the second temple. This stone chair is a work of art with the Aramaic inscription, "Seat of Moshe" which was used for the rabbis as they taught the Torah on behalf or with the authority of Moshe.

*(Yeshua confirmed) The teachers of the law and the Pharisees sit in Moses's seat **in Matthew 23:2 NIV.***

TABLE OF CONTENTS

INTRODUCTION

*T*here are certain advantages I have as a Hebrew (Jewish) man from the priestly tribe of Levy, born and raised in the land of Israel. I have an understanding of the Hebrew idioms, customs and language that are not well understood by most students of the Bible.

I have lived the life of a Hebrew in the land God promised to Avraham, Yitzhak and Ya'akov (Abraham, Isaac and Jacob). I have rubbed shoulders with the people of my forefathers who have preserved the Word of God until today. My upbringing has been particularly useful to me in understanding the New Testament.

If one has been brought up in close contact with the Jewish liturgy, the ceremonies of the Jewish religious year, the rabbinical literature, as well as the overall Jewish moral and cultural ideology, many aspects of the New Testament are familiar and understandable — particularly the Gospels.

This book will not set well, nor will it score high marks among the Bible students and theologians whose minds are seared with established church doctrines and fused with the pagan mentality that existed before churches were established.

"It is Old Testament!" they will claim. "It's for the Jews. The Gentiles have the New Testament." This book, however, may register better with open-minded people seeking to find the truth from a historical, geographical, cultural and scriptural Hebraic point of view.

Many people tend to forget that Shaul (Paul) was a Jew whose teachings never contradicted the Torah, which are God's original teachings and instructions given to Moshe (Moses). He never converted to another religion nor attempted to start a new religion; he was bound by the Law of Moses.

> *Moses writes this about the righteousness that is by the law: "The person who does these things will live by them"* **(Romans 10:5 NIV).**

> *After this, we started on our way up to Jerusalem. Some of the disciples from Caesarea accompanied us and brought us to the home of Mnason, where we were to stay. He was a man from Cyprus and one of the early disciples. When we arrived at Jerusalem, the brothers and sisters received us warmly. The next day Paul and the rest of us went to see James, and all the elders were present. Paul greeted them and reported in detail what God had done among the Gentiles through his ministry. When they heard this, they praised God. Then they said to Paul: "You see, brother, how many thousands of Jews have believed, and all of them are zealous for the law. They have been informed that you teach all the Jews who live among the Gentiles to turn away from Moses, telling them not to circumcise their children or live according to our customs"* **(Acts 21:15-21 NIV).**

Acts 21:15-21 was written after Shaul wrote the letter to the Galatians. This clearly reveals Shaul was an observer of the Torah. Shaul's teaching in Galatians concerning the leading of the spirit and freedom from the law is commonly misunderstood. The authority of the law was not somehow challenged or abolished for believers in Yeshua (Jesus) nor did some spirit that may contradict the written Word supersede the Torah.

We need to remember that *spirit* in Hebrew is *Ruach*, and every time God speaks or creates He does so by His spirit or Ruach. Some additional meanings of spirit include mind, wind, speech, word and

Torah. Therefore when a person lives by the dictates of Torah he is led by God's Ruach or the mind, spirit or word.

> *And the Lord God formed man of the dust of the ground, and* **breathed into his nostrils** *the breath of life; and man become a living soul (**Genesis 2:7**).*

> *And with that he* **breathed on them** *and said, "Receive the Holy Spirit" (**John 20:22**).*

> *Let this mind (**the breathed of Yeshua, His spirit**) be in you, which was also in Yeshua (**Philippians 2:5 NIV**).*

The spirit of Yeshua is the mind of Yeshua. The mind or spirit of Yeshua is the mind of His Father. When we utter words, we are revealing whose spirit or mind we have. We either have the spirit of the world or the spirit of God, which is the Holy Spirit.

> *And grieve not the Holy Spirit [**mind**] of God, whereby ye are sealed unto the day of redemption (**Ephesians 4:30 KJV**).*

When God spoke to the patriarchs, He spoke through His spirit, the wind of His words; when He wrote the Ten Commandments He wrote them through His spirit; when He spoke to Moshe face to face He spoke to him of His spirit. When we attempt to deny the written words or the command from the Torah (Pentateuch), we deny God's spirit.

Does the Holy Spirit have a spirit? The Bible never mentions the spirit of the Holy Spirit. God the Father has a spirit and He Himself also is spirit:

> *For it is not ye that speak, but the Spirit of your Father which also speaketh in you (**Matthew 10:20 KJV**).*

When Yeshua was tempted in the wilderness, the only spirit He used was the written spirit, the Torah. He answered the attacks of the enemy saying, "it is written," then quoted from the Torah the specific law he would be breaking if he followed the enemy's directives. If the written spirit (mind) was good enough for the Son of God, why is it not good enough for us? Are we helpless when attacked by the enemy because we are not using our obedience to the Torah as our defense?

God is spirit and every word from Him comes from His spirit and His mind. Every word He speaks is spirit, which becomes Scripture or the written word, *davar*; from the Hebrew word *dibber*, which is *to speak, to utter*. Shaul was right about Galatians when he argued the following:

> *So I say, live by the Spirit [**Scripture**] and you will not gratify the desires of the sinful nature. For the sinful nature desires what is contrary to the Spirit [**Scripture**] and the Spirit [**Scripture**] what is contrary to the sinful nature. They are in conflict with each other, so that you do not do what you want. But if you are led by the spirit [**mind of God which is evident in Scripture**] you are not under the law (**Galatians 5:16-18 NIV**).*

Nothing speaks or reveals more than the written Word of God. The Scriptures teach us the will of God is the spirit of God. Anyone who relies on feelings and describes it as being led by the spirit of God is open to deception. Who decides what feelings are of the spirit of God or of the spirit of the devil? One can play this game at will, but nothing can be more evident than the *davar* or the written Word of God. *Davar* is of the same root word that describes the Ten Commandments that were given from God to Moshe on Mount Sinai. The Ten Commandments were called **Eser Dibrot,** or *ten words*.

> *Do not merely listen to the word, and so deceive yourselves.* ***Do what it says****. Anyone who listens to the word but does not do what it says is like a man who looks at his face in a mirror and, after looking at himself, goes away and immediately forgets what he looks like. But the man who looks intently into the perfect law that gives freedom, and continues to do*

*this, not forgetting what he has heard, but doing it-he will be blessed in what he does (**James 1:22-25 NIV**).*

Is the above Scripture confusing or hard to understand? It shouldn't be. The emphasis and substance of what is being said is very clear.

Do what the **Word of God** commands!

Ya'acov (James or Jacob), the brother of Christ, is saying to listen to the *Word*. The *Word* in this passage refers to the Scriptures. Which word or Scripture is Ya'acov referring to? The Torah, the Prophets and the Writings.

xvii

THE PURPOSE OF THIS BOOK

*M*y reasons for writing this book are many. Primarily, I wanted to address the perceptions and reactions of two different groups of people when it comes to Shaul's writings. Many Jews and Gentiles know or perceive Shaul as the one who did away with the law, as if he had such authority. It is unfortunate that Shaul shares his letters from a Greek philosophical mindset. His words are often misunderstood or twisted, which Shimon (Peter) specifically cautioned about in **2 Peter**.

> *Bear in mind that our Lord's patience means salvation, just as our dear brother Paul also wrote you with the wisdom that God gave him. He writes the same way in all his letters, speaking in them of these matters.* ***His letters contain some things that are hard to understand, which ignorant and unstable people distort, as they do the other Scriptures, to their own destruction (2 Peter 3:15-16 NIV).***

I want to show my Hebrew and Gentile brothers that Shaul kept the Torah, taught on it at length and attempted to teach the Gentiles of his generation to do the same. More importantly, I want the readers to understand that Shaul is human like the rest of us and made mistakes. Not only have his words been twisted, but they have also been taken as absolute without interpretation, as if he made no mistakes and was something more than a man. The Gentiles have elevated Shaul above that of Yeshua the Son of God. Shaul never had the authority to arbitrarily wipe away the laws of Torah by virtue of Yeshua's death. Even if Shaul taught that we were no longer bound to the law, Yeshua said quite the opposite and it is His words that must prevail.

Shaul was elected to speak to the Gentiles, but he still had to give a full report to Ya'acov (James) the brother of Yeshua who was president of the Sanhedrin. Shaul was under authority and was held accountable for his teachings. Shaul could not teach anything that could be perceived as contrary to the Torah without facing excommunication resulting in banishment from Jerusalem and worship in the temple. The fact that Shaul retained his credentials as a pharisaic rabbi until the day of his execution proves he did not teach or start a new religion but was true to his upbringing in Judaism. Any deviation from true Judaism and the Sanhedrin would have stripped him of his title of rabbi.

When I sat down to write this book I was not looking for people to agree with me. My goal was to get people to understand the Scriptures in the proper light with the Old Testament as the foundation of Biblical interpretation. Many teachers have done a great injustice to Shaul and those they have influenced over the years. I have made every effort to use information relevant from history and Biblical Scriptures to reinforce my statements. Ultimately it will have to be the spirit of Adonai (God) to give understanding of these truths. Sadly, we must plow through nearly two thousand years of false teaching and anti-Semitism to determine how the Gentiles — who are grafted into Israel — are to apply God's commandments to their lives.

There is nothing the Son of God said in the New Testament during his lifetime that was new. All of what Yeshua said can be found in the Torah, the prophets and the writings. When He spoke, there was no debate. It was very clear that the Torah (commandments) was perfect. It is perfect and will forever be perfect, applying to all men.

*The **law of the LORD is perfect**, refreshing the soul. The statutes of the LORD are trustworthy, making wise the simple (**Psalm 19:7 KJV**).*

*But whoever looks intently into the **perfect law** that **gives freedom**, and continues in it not forgetting what they have heard, **but doing it** they will be blessed in what they do (**James 1:25 NIV**).*

*Your righteousness is an everlasting righteousness, and Your law is truth (**Psalm 119:142 KJV**).*

If the law of God is perfect and everlasting how, then, can it come to an end with Yeshua? If that is the case, then it was neither righteous nor everlasting. We need to view the Torah through the eyes of first-century believers in Messiah Yeshua. Why? History testifies that shortly after the apostles died, the Greco-Roman mentality and way of worship infiltrated the new sect of believers in Yeshua; anti-Semitism distorted how the true body of Messiah should worship.

Remember, Yeshua is our example, not Paul or anyone else for that matter! My mission is for people to understand the Scriptures in order to form their opinion based on the evidence of Scripture. My comments are based on scriptural and historical evidence. All the above information is to establish a platform by which to understand Shaul. To let us know what took place two thousand years ago and what established Shaul's style of Hebrew teachings.

LEGALISM OR LAW

*M*any people confuse legalism (man's traditions, dogmas and doctrines) with the laws of the Torah, which are God-given laws.

*These are the things God has revealed to us by his Spirit [**Torah**]. The Spirit searches all things, even the deep things of God. For who knows a person's thoughts except their own spirit [**knowledge of Scripture**] within them? In the same way no one knows the thoughts of God except the Spirit of God [**Scripture is the word that comes out of God's mouth; words of God are the spirit of God.**] What we have received is not the spirit [**Word**] of the world, but the Spirit [**Word**] who is from God, so that we may understand what God has freely given to us. [**Torah**] This is what we speak, not in words taught us by human wisdom but in words taught by the Spirit, [**mind of God, Scripture**] explaining spiritual realities with Spirit-taught words. The person without the Spirit does not accept the things that come from the Spirit of God but considers them foolishness, and cannot understand them because they are discerned only through the Spirit (**1 Corinthians 2:10-14 NIV**).*

*Now the overseer must be above reproach, the husband of but one wife, temperate, self-controlled, respectable, hospitable, able to teach, not given to drunkenness, not violent but gentle, not quarrelsome, not a lover of money. He must manage his own family well and see that his children obey him with proper respect. (If anyone does not know how to manage his own family, how can he take care of God's church?) He must not be a recent convert, or he may become conceited and fall under the same judgment as the devil. He must also have a good reputation with outsiders, so that he will not fall into disgrace and into the devil's trap (**1 Timothy 3:2-7 NIV**).*

According to Shaul's writings, a person desiring the position of overseer must:

1. *Be a man.*
2. *Be above reproach.*
3. *Be the husband of one wife.*
4. *Be temperate.*
5. *Be self-controlled.*
6. *Be respectable.*
7. *Be hospitable.*
8. *Be able to teach.*
9. *Not given to drunkenness.*
10. *Be Non-violent.*
11. *Be gentle.*
12. *Not quarrelsome.*
13. *Not love money.*
14. *Manage his family well.*
15. *Make sure his children give proper respect.*
16. *Not a recent convert.*
17. *Have a good reputation with the outside community.*

These are requirements for one who seeks to be an overseer or leader. They are borne of laws or rules that must be followed. They are detailed, specific and unbending qualifications.

24

Where did these requirements originate? Did Shaul just make these up out of thin air? What guidelines did he use to determine what would make a suitable overseer? Some form or standard had to be followed. These qualifications were derived from the Word of God, the word or spirit given to Moshe, to the Levites, the prophets and even the kings of Israel.

When Shaul spoke of being *under the law* or the *works of the law*, he was speaking against the burdens and traditions being added to the Torah by the teachers of the law. He was never at any point against keeping God's Torah. There is no Hebrew word for the concept of *legalism* or being a *legalist*. This is why Shaul's writings are hindered in his attempt to explain to the Gentiles that legalism was *not* what God intended. Shaul was not teaching against Torah observance for the believers of Yeshua. Rather, he was being careful in his language to make it clear that the Torah was not given by God for men to add or subtract from in order to suit their preferences and lifestyles. Nor was the Torah given in order for men to create a system of traditions or burdens for personal gain or power.

There are many people who like to insist there is no explicit requirements in the New Testament to keep the commandments in the Torah, or maintain adherence to the conditions set forth in the old covenant. Yet Yeshua states along with the writers of the New Testament very clearly the following.

Do we, then, nullify the law by this faith? Not at all! Rather,

*we uphold the law (**Romans 3:31 NIV**).*

*Would you discredit my justice? Would you condemn me to justify yourself (**Job 40:8 NIV**)?*

*It is written: "Man does not live on bread alone, but by every word that comes from the mouth of God" (**Matthew 4:4 NIV**).*

The very Son of God—the one who created heaven and earth— is saying, *"Men must live by **every word that comes from the mouth of God**."* The laws of God come from the mouth of God. Did the word of God come forth only in the New Testament or is it eternal, existing even before creation? The book of Genesis records the Lord saying, *"Let there be light."* God's words proceed out of His spirit. When God speaks, His words are active. They are wind, the spirit and the law. Everything God speaks is a command; when He speaks, something happens.

I routinely ask believers if they think God will ever flood the earth again. Their response to my question is, "No." I then will ask them, "Why?" They often paraphrase **Genesis 9:11-16** as their answer, "Because in the Bible, God said He wouldn't do that again."

> *I establish my covenant with you: Never again will all life be destroyed by the waters of a flood; never again will there be a flood to destroy the earth. And God said, "This is the sign of the covenant I am making between me and you and every living creature with you, a covenant for all generations to come: I have set my rainbow in the clouds, and it will be the sign of the covenant between me and the earth. Whenever I bring clouds over the earth and the rainbow appears in the clouds, I will remember my covenant between me and you and all living creatures of every kind. Never again will the waters become a flood to destroy all life. Whenever the rainbow appears in the clouds, I will see it and remember the everlasting covenant between God and all living creatures of every kind on the earth" (Genesis 9:11-16 NIV).*

Why do we believe God will never flood the earth again on the basis of just one statement in Genesis, yet over fifty passages reference that God's laws are forever? Do we discard all the promises from the prophets in the Old Testament regarding the birth, death and resurrection of Yeshua? Do we discard the promises of redemption and restoration of God's kingdom from the prophets in the Old Testament? No, we hold on to those promises. The same prophets who predicted the coming Mashiach (Messiah) spoke warnings against those who did not keep the laws of God. Moshe, as well as these same prophets, spoke of God's promise to curse all those who disobey Him.

Israel did not keep the commandments of God and they were cursed. They were exiled from their homes and suffered gruesome deaths. Their children were raised as slaves in foreign lands, thrown to the lions, forced into furnaces and hung from gallows.

> *You rebuke the arrogant,* **who are cursed and who stray from your commands** *(Psalm 119:21 NIV).*

> *Tell them that this is what the LORD, the God of Israel, says:* **"Cursed is the man who does not obey the terms of this covenant**, *the terms I commanded your forefathers when I brought them out of Egypt, out of the iron-smelting furnace." I said, "Obey me and do everything I command you, and you will be my people, and I will be your God"* **(Jeremiah 11:3-4 NIV).**

> *All who rely on observing the law are under a curse, for it is written:* **"Cursed is everyone who does not continue to do everything written in the Book of the Law"** *(Galatians 3:10 NIV).*

If Shaul taught the people, Jews or Gentiles, to deny or forsake the law, then both He the teacher and the ones practicing are cursed based on what Adonai commanded Moshe in **Deuteronomy 27:26**:

> *Cursed is anyone who does not uphold the words of this law by carrying them out* **(Deuteronomy 27:26 NIV).**

What is the purpose of Shaul boasting on his Jewish ancestry and upbringing in Philippians 3:5?

> *Circumcised on the eighth day, of the people of Israel, of the tribe of Benjamin, a Hebrew of Hebrews; in regard to the law, a Pharisee;* **(Philippians 3:5 NIV)**

Why would he emphasize this fact only to turn around and deny the Torah by stating it was only for the Jews and the law is fulfilled with in the death of Yeshua?

Proclaiming to do away with the law that gives you authority is like climbing a tree and cutting down the very branch holding you up. The Torah is the umbilical cord that has sustained the Jewish people for thousands of years; it is not only the trunk of the tree, but the root as well. The New Testament grew as a branch on the Old Testament tree. The existence of the New Testament and its relevance depend upon the existence and validation of the Torah as the supreme Word of God.

There is nothing the Son of God said in the New Testament during his lifetime that was new to the Torah, prophets and writings. Shaul continued to boast about his Jewishness to emphasize that he was Torah observant. It was his Torah observance that allowed him to understand Yeshua and it was his Torah observance that led him to Rome where he was beheaded.

A MANUAL BETWEEN
GOD AND MANKIND

*T*he letter to the Romans is Shaul's work in the synagogue (not church) of Rome where Jews and Gentiles met to study the Tanakh (Old Testament). The Tanakh was the only Biblical text available at that time. There were no New Testament writings for over one hundred years after the disciples' work, therefore, neither Shaul nor the disciples of Yeshua could use or quote from them.

The New Testament letters were not completed until 150 AD, roughly eighty-three years after Shaul's death in Rome. It wasn't until early 300 AD when the New Testament became universally accepted as a canon. Yet the recognition of these writings as being authoritative by the orthodox Christians was not till 695 AD, that was six hundred twenty-five years after the death of Shaul. Historically, traditionally and culturally it is well established that the disciples who continued the work of Yeshua never used the New Testament. They used what was available to them, what we call the Old Testament. Up until 100 AD, the Tanakh was **never addressed as the Old Testament**.

Tanakh is a Hebrew acronym or abbreviated word for three distinct collections of books:

Torah (T), the five books of Moshe
Nevi'im (N), the prophets
Ktuvim (K), for the Writings

The Old Testament is broken down into the following segments:

- The **Torah**, which means *teaching*. These books are the teaching books known as the five books of Moshe, which are Genesis, Exodus, Leviticus, Numbers and Deuteronomy.
- The **Nevi'im** meaning "prophets" the historical and prophetic books which include Joshua, Judges, I Samuel, II Samuel, I Kings, II Kings, Isaiah, Jeremiah, Ezekiel, Hosea, Joel, Amos, Obadiah, Jonah, Micah, Nahum, Habakkuk, Zephaniah, Haggai, Zechariah and Malachi.
- The **Ktuvim**, which are *the writings* and are considered the poetic books. These books are Psalms, Proverbs, Job, Song of Songs, Ruth, Lamentations, Ecclesiastes, Esther, Daniel, Ezra and Nehemiah, I Chronicles and II Chronicles.

Many Christians today try to interpret the Old Testament through understanding the New Testament. We must do the exact opposite. The Old Testament forms the foundation for everything you read in the New Testament. Shaul is the person he is because of the Old Testament. His life centered on the Torah and he was molded by its teachings.

To understand the New Testament one must first start at the beginning in Genesis. It is in the beginning we understand how we fell into sin and the effect that sin had on us, on creation and on our relationship with our Father in heaven. It is at the beginning we will understand how to get out of sin, who will redeem us and where the Savior will appear. All this has to be understood before we can accept the person from Beit Lechem (Bethlehem, house of bread) as our Mashiach (Messiah). Without the Old Testament, what evidence do we use to establish Yeshua of the New Testament as the Mashiach? There have been many throughout history that claimed to be a messiah or savior and some counterfeit messiahs who even claimed to be The Mashiach.

The entire Bible (*Byblos* or *library* in Greek) is not a Christian book in origin. It is a Hebrew (Jewish) book given to the Hebrew people, handed down initially by oral tradition. The sons of Noah, **Shem, Ham** and **Yafet** carried the knowledge of sacred teachings. The genealogy of Shem is recorded in **Genesis 11:10.**

> *This is the account of Shem's family line. Two years after the flood, when Shem was 100 years old, he became the father of Arphaxad (**Genesis 11:10**).*

Shem carries the legacy of Havel (Able) and that of Shet (Seth) through Abraham, King David and Yeshua the Messiah, who came from his line. Shem has become synonymous in Judaism as one of the names of God, **Ha' Shem** became known as The Name, or the God of Shem. Shem, the father of the *Hebrew soul*, was committed to the Laws of Adonai, while the other brothers claimed a different path to God. The descendants of **Yafet**, the older brother, created their version of the Hebrew Tanakh and called it *Catechism*, which is a central book of Catholicism.

Zacharias Ursinus (1534-1583), the primary author of the Heidelberg Catechism:

> The Greek word *kataecaesis* is derived from kataeceoh, as kataecismos is from kataecidzoh. Both words, according to their common signification, mean to sound, to resound, to instruct by word of mouth, and to repeat the sayings of another. Kataeceoh more properly, however, means to teach the first principles and rudiments of some particular doctrine. As applied to the doctrine of the church and as understood when thus used, it means to teach the first principles of the Christian religion, in which sense it occurs in Luke 1:4, Acts 18:25, Gal. 6:6. Hence, catechisation in its most general and comprehensive sense, means the first brief and elementary instruction which is given by word of mouth in relation to the rudiments of any particular doctrine; but, as used by the church, it signifies a system of instruction relating to the first principles of the Christian religion, designed for the

ignorant and unlearned. The system of catechising, therefore, includes a short, simple, and plain exposition and rehearsal of the Christian doctrine, deduced from the writings of the prophets and apostles, and arranged in the form of questions and answers, adapted to the capacity and comprehension of the ignorant and unlearned; or it is a brief summary of the doctrine of the prophets and apostles, communicated orally to such as are unlearned, which they again are required to repeat.

Ham on the other hand, interpreted large portions of the Hebrew Tanakh, which **evolved into Islam** five hundred years after the establishment of Catholicism. The **Quran**, meaning, "to recite" is **Islam's holy book**. The Protestants, a branch out of the Catholic Church, used the Hebrew Tanach and called it the Christian Bible, or the **Holy Bible**. It **was not** the Hebrew people who named it the **Holy Bible**, rather the Gentile Christians who declared unanimously that the entire book, Old and New Testaments, Genesis to Revelation are holy books given by God. Reading the New Testament only, without ever reading or understanding the Old Testament, will leave gaps in specific areas necessary for a strong walk with God. Our relationship to Adonai is based on the knowledge and clear understanding of what God gave us in the Old Testament. The Torah specifically forms an important base for God and man and their relationship to one another.

Shaul does not need to interpret the Old Testament in the same manner that we do today. We must study the languages, historical data, and archeological artifacts to interpret the Old Testament. Shaul had mastered and understood the Torah because he lived during that time period in Israel and was tutored under Rabbi Gamliel, one of the greatest rabbis of that day. He read the original manuscripts of the Torah, Nevi'im and Ktuvim (Torah, prophets and writings). The idea that he was trying to understand or interpret the Tanakh as a teacher of the law (as he boasted) is absurd.

In the New Testament Shaul is communicating to the Greeks in their own language using the original Hebrew text. He was assigned to take the Good News to the Gentiles using the only Testament available at that time. Shaul uses direct quotes, allusions, cultural references, allegories and other references that would make sense to his intended audience, the Greeks. He was attempting to convey the importance of Yeshua to his Greek-minded audience, using every possible means available to help them understand. He was not binding himself to a particular method of interpretation, and he was not interpreting the Tanakh. He was teaching it as one who understood it deeply. He was revealing Yeshua from the Old Testament.

Shaul used one form of teaching when addressing the Jews, one with which he was very familiar. In contrast, when teaching the Greeks, he was in unfamiliar territory and therefore used whatever common ground he could find. When we understand the challenges that Shaul had in teaching the Greeks, we can then understand he never twisted or perverted the Old Testament Scripture to accomplish a different understanding of the Torah. It is precisely because of Shaul's challenges in reaching the Greeks that we should be careful not to interpret his methods. Most of us are not Greek and cannot relate to the historical period they lived in, nor understand the full implications of their pagan lifestyles and mindset.

Shaul had more freedom in his expression of the original text than we will ever possess simply because we are so far removed from the knowledge Shaul had. Thus, we have a far narrower understanding of the authority of the written word than he did. It was new for Shaul to open the door to the Gentiles and welcome them into the covenant of Avraham, Yitzhak and Ya'akov. He devised a method that would be captivating to the Gentiles and would encourage them to reject their false idols that were physical and submit to the one invisible God of the Hebrews.

The culture of that day was polytheistic and the pagans had many idols. They did not widely accept the idea of a singular, invisible God. They took pride in crafting their gods from wood, stone, silver, gold and bronze. The God of the Hebrews was not visible and they certainly never heard His voice. Except the few individuals who were chosen by God to deliver His word, the God of the Hebrews could only be touched by blind faith in His Torah.

We are at a disadvantage today compared to Shaul. We are studying and dealing with secondhand information. Here we are thousands of years later, attempting to understand what it is Moshe, the Levites, the prophets and the kings of Israel wrote in the Hebrew Scriptures. We must rely on their writings and understanding of the Old Testament Scriptures at a simple level, as opposed to interpreting what we think Shaul meant when speaking to a Greek audience.

Our job is not to interpret, but to understand the revealed word and declare it. To achieve this, we must first understand the Scriptures from the original language, Genesis to Malachi, and understand the customs and idioms of the people who wrote and preserved the Bible. Once that has been achieved, we can then bring the New Testament writings and those of Shaul into harmony with the Torah, the prophets and the writings.

THE BRANCH

*I*n Genesis 4, we see Adam's sons; Cain, means bought with a price and Abel, means breath or spirit. In verse 25, another son was born to replace Abel who was slain by his brother Cain. He was named Seth/Shet, means, "the planting of a seed." This planting of a seed was of the same spirit or in the place of Abel.

In the New Testament we see that John the Baptist received the spirit of Elijah. Does that mean that Elijah was reincarnated in another form and another person? No, spirit is also mind, so the mind or the knowledge that Elijah had was passed down to John the Baptist in a divine manner.

> *The spirit of the Sovereign Lord is on me, because the Lord has anointed me to proclaim good news to the poor. He has sent me to bind up the brokenhearted, to proclaim freedom for the captives and release from darkness for the prisoners (**Isaiah 61:1 NIV**).*

Isaiah 61:1 speaks of Yeshua, when He claims to have the spirit of God upon Him. He does not claim to be God, the Father. He only has the knowledge of the Father. He has the same purpose, same will, character and principles of His Father. There are other similar shadows in the Scriptures that may be puzzling to many unless they are schooled in the Hebraic Scriptures (Torah) and learned in their ways of study.

Yeshua Under Authority

"By myself I can do nothing; I judge only as I hear, and my judgment is just, for I seek not to please myself but him who sent me.

"If I testify about myself, my testimony is not true. There is another who testifies in my favor and I know that his testimony about me is true.

"You have sent to John and he has testified to the truth. Not that I accept human testimony, but I mention it that you may be saved. John was a lamp that burned and gave light, and you chose for a time to enjoy his light.

"I have testimony weightier than that of John. For the works that the Father has given me to finish—the very works that I am doing—testify that the Father has sent me. And the Father who sent me has himself testified concerning me. You have never heard his voice nor seen his form, nor does his word dwell in you, for you do not believe the one he sent. You study the Scriptures diligently because you think that in them you have eternal life. These are the very Scriptures that testify about me, yet you refuse to come to me to have life.

"I do not accept glory from human beings, but I know you. I know that you do not have the love of God in your hearts. I have come in my Father's name, and you do not accept me; but if someone else comes in his own name, you will accept him. How can you believe since you accept glory from one another, but do not seek the glory that comes from the only God?

"But do not think I will accuse you before the Father. Your accuser is Moses, on whom your hopes are set. If you believed Moses, you would believe me, for he wrote about me. But since you do not believe what he wrote, how are you going to believe what I say?" (***John 5:30-47 NIV***)

Concerning the City of Nazareth in Matthew:

*And he came and dwelt in a city called Nazareth: that it might be fulfilled which was spoken by the prophets, He shall be called a Nazarene (**Matthew 2:23 KJV**).*

*And when they had performed all things according to the law (Torah) of the Lord, they returned into Galilee, to their own city Nazareth (**Luke 2:39 KJV**).*

When you read the above verses, it would appear that the focus is on the city of Nazareth rather than on Yeshua. The problem is that the city of Nazareth is never mentioned in the Old Testament or Apocrypha. Did Matityahu (Matthew) make a mistake connecting Nazareth to a fulfilled prophecy? The relevance of Nazareth is not about the city itself, but the fulfillment of Old Testament prophecies found in Jeremiah, Isaiah and Zechariah regarding Yeshua Ha' Mashiach.

The connection is to the Hebrew words, *Tzemach* and *netzer*. Both words are used as branch, sprout or shoot in the English translations of the Holy Bible. *Netzer* is where Nazareth originates from in English. The allusion of *netzer* is of an olive tree that has been razed to the ground eventually followed by a shoot or branch erupting from the dead stock. Hence, a *netzer* comes forth from the stock (stump), the stock being King David. Although the kingdom of David has been razed to the ground, many years later a sprout shot forth out of the ground in Beit-Lechem Judea from King David's dynasty.

*And there shall come forth a shoot out of the stock of Jesse, and a branch [**Netzer**], but of his roots shall bear fruit (**Isaiah 11:1 ASV**).*

*"Behold, the days are coming," declares the Lord, "When I will raise up for David a righteous branch [**Tzemach**]; and He will reign as king and act wisely and do justice and righteousness in the land" (**Jeremiah 33:14-15 KJV**).*

37

The use of *netzer* and *Tzemach* in the Old Testament both refer to Yeshua whom God would raise up to bring justice, righteousness and peace to His people. Both words are used with the same intent to identify Yeshua as the king from the line of David whom God did finally raised up to restore His people.

> *Now listen, Joshua the high priest, you and your friends who are sitting in front of you—indeed they are men **who are a symbol**, for behold, **I am going to bring in My servant the Branch [Netzer] (Zechariah 3:8 NASB).***

> *In that day shall the branch **[Tzemach]** of the LORD be beautiful and glorious, and the fruit of the earth shall be excellent and comely for them that are escaped of Israel **(Isaiah 4:2 KJV).***

While the plan of God is about the restoration of Israel, one thing does stand out in this story. A common enemy razed both the King (Yeshua) and Israel to the ground.

> *"The days are coming," declares the LORD, "when I will **raise up to David a righteous Branch, a King** who will reign wisely and do what is just and right in the land. In his days Judah will be saved and Israel will live in safety. This is the name by which he will be called: The LORD Our Righteousness'" **(Jeremiah 23:5-6 NIV).***

> *It is because of him that you are in Christ Jesus, who has become for us wisdom from God—that is, our righteousness, holiness and redemption **(1 Corinthians 1:30 NIV).***

The Romans physically killed Yeshua. The same Romans physically razed the Jewish people to the ground in 70 AD. They were dispersed to the four corners of the world for two thousand years. Just as Yeshua was raised on the third day, the Jewish people had a miraculous resurrection on the third day in 1948.

*When they came together in Galilee, he said to them, 'The Son of Man is going to be betrayed into the hands of men. They will kill him, and on the third day he will be raised to life.' And the disciples were filled with grief (**Matthew 17:22-23 NIV**).*

*Come, let us return to the LORD. He has torn us to pieces but he will heal us; he has injured us but he will bind up our wounds. After two days he will revive us; on the third day he will restore us, that we may live in his presence (**Hosea 6:1-2 NIV**).*

The hand of the Lord was on me, and he brought me out by the Spirit of the Lord and set me in the middle of a valley; it was full of bones. He led me back and forth among them, and I saw a great many bones on the floor of the valley, bones that were very dry. He asked me, "Son of man, can these bones live?" I said, "Sovereign Lord, you alone know." Then he said to me, "Prophesy to these bones and say to them, 'Dry bones, hear the word of the Lord! This is what the Sovereign Lord says to these bones: I will make breath enter you, and you will come to life. I will attach tendons to you and make flesh come upon you and cover you with skin; I will put breath in you, and you will come to life. Then you will know that I am the Lord.'" So I prophesied as I was commanded. And as I was prophesying, there was a noise, a rattling sound, and the bones came together, bone to bone. I looked, and tendons and flesh appeared on them and skin covered them, but there was no breath in them. Then he said to me, "Prophesy to the breath; prophesy, son of man, and say to it, 'This is what the Sovereign Lord says: Come, breath, from the four winds and breathe into these slain, that they may live.'" So I prophesied as he commanded me, and breath entered them; they came to life and stood up on their feet—a vast army. Then he said to me: "Son of man, these bones are the people of Israel. They say, 'Our bones are dried up and our hope is gone; we are cut off.' Therefore prophesy *and say to them: 'This is what the Sovereign Lord says: My people, I am going to open your graves and bring you up from them; I will bring you back to the land of Israel. Then you, my people, will know that I am the Lord, when I open your graves and bring you up from them. I will put my spirit in you and you will live, and I will settle you in your own land. Then you will know that I the Lord have spoken, and I have done it, declares the Lord'" (**Ezekiel 37:1-14 NIV**).*

Hosea 6:1-2 and **Ezekiel 37:1-14** were fulfilled in 1948 with the establishment of the state of Israel into a formidable nation. After being wiped out for two thousand years and against all odds, Israel was restored back to their ancestral homeland and their Hebrew language, reminiscent of the exodus from Egypt.

*But the Lord hath taken you, and brought you forth out of the iron furnace, even out of Egypt, to be unto him a people of inheritance, as ye are this day (**Deuteronomy 4:20 KJV**).*

God saved and restored His people from the ovens of Europe. Once again we see the effect from Yafet and Ham upon their brother Shem. The prophets used various metaphors to refer to the anticipated revival of the righteous King, which would replace the corrupt kings of the day. Isaiah, Jeremiah and Zechariah used the word *branch* as a metaphor for the new king that God would raise up from the line of David.

Yeshua was born in Beit-Lechem (Bethlehem) meaning, "the house of bread." The town of Ephrata means "sheep and shepherds." Sheep and shepherds refer to the people of Israel. He was raised in the town called Nazareth (Netzer), the place of the fish. Fish speaks of the people of the world. **Netzer**, a shoot from the line of the beloved King David is connected to Nazareth, a small town that is almost unknown and is identified with Yeshua's upbringing. Beit-Lechem also was relatively unknown yet identified as being King David and Yeshua's birthplace.

Both cities reveal Yeshua's role to humanity, **Netzer**, or Nazareth describes Yeshua as the offshoot of the Davidic dynasty to rule as a king in the end days. Beit Lechem describes Him as the house of bread. In Him, we find sustenance and satisfaction for eternal life. Beit-Lechem, the house of bread and the place of the sheep, describes where He came from. The Lamb of God came from the fold of sheep (Israel). He was raised in Nazareth, the place of fish. His mission is to fish for the people of the world.

All of this is Matityahu's (Matthew's) way of proclaiming Yeshua as the Messiah! He is referring to points in history rather than physical landmarks. He is revealing Yeshua from the prophets of the Old Testament that promised the **netzer**, the branch that is the promised Mashiach. It is unlikely that Isaiah, Jeremiah, Zechariah or any of the prophets were thinking about the city of Nazareth when they wrote about the netzer. They were not predicting anything about the city of Nazareth; they were writing about the last righteous king known as **Netzer Ishai**, the root of Jesse, who will rule Israel and the world.

> *A shoot will come up from the stump of Jesse; from his roots a Branch will fruit (**Isaiah 11:1 NIV**).*

Nothing could be more convincing than the style Matityahu used to reveal Yeshua to the Hebrews. He used a common method of teaching using allegorical associations to show Yeshua in the prophecies. His teaching style essentially connected the dots via association using the information that had been passed from one generation to the next. Nothing he presented stood on its own; his revelations were connected to the revelations of the past. Everything had a precedent, a witness to bear out his revelations about Yeshua being the Mashiach.

Matityahu's style is reminiscent of the way teaching is done in the synagogues of today, which is vastly different from how churches teach. On any given Sunday, you never know what a certain church will be teaching. Compare that to the synagogues around the world, which teach the same Torah portion for that week. No matter where a Jew travels he can go to any synagogue in the world and he will know the Torah for that week. The teaching does not change from one synagogue to the next. This method of synchronized study creates a uniform platform that increases comprehension and clarity, creating a deeper and universal understanding collectively since everyone is on the same page. This bonds people to a common cause and unites them to the patriarchs and the covenant they have with God. The uniformity of Torah portion study informs and prepares the people regarding holy events like Passover, trumpets, or tabernacles. Nothing can unify a people better then the study style of dividing the Torah into fifty-two or fifty-six portions for the year depending if it is a leap year or not.

WHO IS SHAUL (PAUL)?

*S*haul's parents were born in Gush Halav in Galilee. During the uprising in Yerushalaim (Jerusalem) they moved to Turkey where his mother raised Shaul until the age of five in Tarsus, Turkey. As was the Jewish custom, his father, a devout Parush, took over teaching his son the Scriptures and traditional writings. At the age of ten years old, his parents sent Shaul to Yerushalaim to attend the rabbinical school of Gamliel. Gamliel was the famous rabbi mentioned in the New Testament.

> *But a Pharisee named Gamliel, a teacher of the law, who was honored by all the people, stood up in the Sanhedrin and ordered that the men be put outside for a little while (**Acts 5:34 NIV**).*

In his mid-twenties, Shaul returned to Tarsus with zeal to teach Torah to the Jews in the diaspora. It was customary for rabbis at that time to have a trade as a second source of income. Shaul became skilled in tent making in addition to teaching the Torah.

According to Luke's record in Acts, Shaul began to persecute the church.

*Shaul began to destroy the church, going from house to house; he dragged off men and women and put them in prison (**Acts: 8:3 NIV**).*

Having warrants for the Christian in Damascus, on the way a bright light engulfed him. A voice calling his name "Shaul, Shaul, why do you persecute me?" Saul responded: "Who are you, Lord (Adoni-Master)?" since Shaul never seen or heard Yeshua he did not know who was calling him. As he neared Damascus on his journey, suddenly a light from heaven flashed around him. He fell to the ground and heard a voice say to him, "Saul, Saul, why do you persecute me?" "Who are you, Lord?" Saul asked. "I am Jesus, whom you are persecuting," he replied. "Now get up and go into the city, and you will be told what you must do." The men traveling with Saul stood there speechless; they heard the sound but did not see anyone. Saul got up from the ground, but when he opened his eyes he could see nothing. So they led him by the hand into Damascus. For three days he was blind, and did not eat or drink anything. In Damascus there was a disciple named Ananias. The Lord called to him in a vision, "Ananias! "Yes, Lord," he answered. The Lord told him, "Go to the house of Judas on Straight Street and ask for a man from Tarsus named Saul, for he is praying. In a vision he has seen a man named Ananias come and place his hands on him to restore his sight." "Lord," Ananias answered, "I have heard many reports about this man and all the harm he has done to your holy people in Jerusalem. And he has come here with authority from the chief priests to arrest all who call on your name." But the Lord said to Ananias, "Go! This man is my chosen instrument to proclaim my name to the Gentiles and their kings and to the people of Israel. I will show him how much he must suffer for my name." Then Ananias went to the house and entered it. Placing his hands on Saul, he said, "Brother Saul, the Lord—Jesus, who appeared to you on the road as you were coming here—has sent me so that you may see again and be filled with the Holy

Spirit." Immediately, something like scales fell from Saul's eyes, and he could see again. He got up and was baptized, and after taking some food, he regained his strength.

*Saul spent several days with the disciples in Damascus. At once he began to preach in the synagogues that Jesus is the Son of God. All those who heard him were astonished and asked, "Isn't he the man who raised havoc in Jerusalem among those who call on this name? And hasn't he come here to take them as prisoners to the chief priests?" Yet Saul grew more and more powerful and baffled the Jews living in Damascus by proving that Jesus is the Messiah (**Acts 9:3-22 NIV**).*

Yeshua directed Shaul to a Levite to pray for him and he was healed. It was a Levite who taught Shaul about Yeshua from the Scriptures in the Tanach, Torah, prophets and the writings. All that Shaul learned from Rabbi Gamliel, all he learned from the temple Levites and all he learned from Chanania the Levite, was based on the Tanach. There is nothing Shaul taught that was contradicting his years of Jewish studies. To the contrary, his eyes were opened for the first time about the Scriptures concerning Yeshua.

There is no mention of Shaul by the respected historian, Yoseph Ben Matityahoo, (Josephus son of Matthias) who was of the tribe of Levy. Yoseph (Josephus) was a contemporary to Shaul. They would have been about the same age and studied under the same reputable Rabbi Gamliel the grandson of Rabbi Hillel, the elder. They both had Roman citizenship and they could travel about the country with no restrictions. In his writings, Yoseph does mention Yochanan Levy (John the Baptist) and even the Essenes from Qumran, yet not a word or hint about Shaul was penned. There is also no mention of Yeshua in Yoseph's work.

It is possible that Yoseph wrote history under the protection of Vespianus in Rome, but there was a period where to be a Notzri (Messianic) was a capital crime punishable by death and that included Roman citizens. Therefore any mention or association with Shaul (Paul) would be a death sentence.

The Confession of Saul

> *Unto me, **who am less than the least of all saints**, is this grace given, that I should preach among the Gentiles the unsearchable riches of Christ. . . (**Ephesians 3:8 KJV**).*

> *For I also am an Israelite, of the seed of Abraham, of the tribe of **Benjamin** (**Romans 11:1 AKJ**).*

> *. . .circumcised on the eighth day, of the people of Israel, of the tribe of Benjamin, a Hebrew of Hebrews; in regard to the law, a Pharisee; (**Philippians 3:5 NIV**).*

Shaul tells us in **Romans 11:1 AKJ**, *"For I also am an Israelite, of the seed of Abraham, of the tribe of **Benjamin**."* Shaul repeats this in **Philippians 3:5 KJV**, saying he is *"of the stock of Israel, of the tribe of Benjamin."* In **Ephesians 3:8 KJV** when Shaul states, *"Unto me, **who am less than the least of all saints**, is this grace given, that I should preach among the Gentiles the unsearchable riches of Christ. . ."* he is speaking in reference to his ancestral tribe.

Shaul was born into a tribe with a bad name, a bad king and a bad reputation. Benyamin was considered the least of all the tribes of Israel, which Shaul referenced in **Ephesians 3:8**. He was up against a great challenge to clean up his tribe's name. Shaul desired to redeem the name of Benyamin. He had much to overcome when he confessed that he came from the least of the tribes. This was spoken in reference to the lineage of his tribe. It was not a humble statement, but a confession of a shameful reality. It is a fact that God wiped out the tribe of Benjamin for their immoral acts and their cruelty. But God preserved the women of Ben 'YAmin to continue the line of the tribe. Shaul knew what he had to do; he had to clean up the reputation of his tribe. He understood what King Shlomo (Solomon) said: *"Better a good name than precious oil (**Ecclesiastes 7:1 ASV**).*

A Deeper Look at Shaul's Tribe

> *Benjamin is a ravenous wolf: in the morning he devours the prey, in the evening he divides the plunder (**Genesis 49: 27 NIV**).*

The story of Ben 'YAmin is unique. In **Genesis 49: 27** Jacob is blessing his sons before his passing. As he blesses his son Ben 'YAmin, the Holy Spirit prompts a prophetic word through Jacob saying that Ben 'YAmin, son of my right hand, is a ravenous wolf. Ben 'YAmin's mother, Rachel, died in childbirth, but not before she named him **Ben 'Oni**, meaning, "son of my sorrow." After Rachel's death, Yaakov changed his name to **Ben 'YAmin**, son of my right hand, although most of the tribe of Ben 'YAmin were left-handed.

Ben 'YAmin caused conflict between Yosef and Ya'acov for the release of his brothers from an Egyptian prison. Moshe inflicted the Egyptians in order to release his brothers Israel from Egypt. In **Judges 3:15-23**, Israelites cried out to the LORD and he gave them a deliverer, Ehud, a left-handed man, the son of Gera, the Benjamite. The tribe had a reputation as being the fiercest fighters of all the tribes in Israel.

In **1 Samuel 9:1, 14:47-52,** the first king of Israel (Shaul) came from the tribe of Ben 'YAmin. He disobeyed God's commands and his Kingship was taken from him and given to David from the Tribe of Yehudah. **Genesis 19:4–11,24,25** tells the story of Sodom, Gomorrah and three joining cities. In the days of Lot, they became perverted and turned to a homosexual lifestyle resulting in the fire from God. This Scripture is relevant and sets the stage for the tribe of Ben 'YAmin.

God sets the record straight for the nation of Israel in the Torah. Learn NOT the way of the pagans and do not practice their immoral lifestyle:

> *Do not lie with a man as one lies with a woman; that is detestable (**Leviticus 18:22 NIV**).*

*Do not be deceived: Neither the sexually immoral nor idolaters nor adulterers nor male prostitutes nor homosexual offenders. . .will inherit the kingdom of God (**1 Corinthians 6:9,10 NIV**).*

*They exchanged the truth about God for a lie, and worshiped and served created things rather than the Creator—who is forever praised. Amen. Because of this, God gave them over to shameful lusts. Even their women exchanged natural sexual relations for unnatural ones. In the same way the men also abandoned natural relations with women and were inflamed with lust for one another. Men committed shameful acts with other men, and received in themselves the due penalty for their error (**Romans 1:25–27 NIV**).*

In the above passages, Paul is referring to both male homosexuality and female lesbianism. Their unnatural sexual behavior is a sin against God, who established the order of sexuality.

Judges 19 and 20 records an incident in the ancient **Benjamite city** of Gibeah that has many similarities to the sin of Sodom. Certain wicked men of the city sought to force a visiting Levite into homosexual acts with them. Resisting their insistent requests, the attackers finally settled for a vicious act of sexual abuse and gang raped the Levite's concubine, resulting in her death. The other tribes of Israel found the crime so repugnant that when the tribe of **Ben 'Yamin** refused to surrender the offenders, they eventually went to war destroying the men from the tribe of **Ben 'YAmin (Judges 19:1-30; 20:1-48).**

Shaul (Paul) the Wolf

*Benjamin is a wolf that ravenous: In the morning he shall devour the prey, and at evening he shall divide the spoil (**Genesis 49:27 ASV**).*

A wolf never goes hungry because he hunts for himself and is cunning; its main interest is to kill. It is strong, a hunter and calculating when hunting. Whom does the Benjamite prophecy speak of when considering the wolf? When digging deeper into Scripture, there are three prominent Benjamites in history who could possibly be the wolf: Shaul, the first king of Israel, Mordechai (Queen Ester's uncle) and Shaul in the New Testament.

(Shaul) King Saul of Israel

The first king of Israel was King Saul (Shaul). He was always in view and at the forefront. He was a very public figure.

> *When you come into the land which the Lord your God is giving you and inherit it and live in it, and you say, "Let us appoint over me a king like all the nation around me," [then] you will appoint over yourself a king whom the Lord your God shall choose. From among your brothers are you to appoint over yourself a king, you may not appoint over yourself a foreigner who is not your bother (**Deuteronomy 17:14-15 NKJV**).*

God predicts that Israel will not want an invisible God, but a physical tangible king like the pagans. God knew that Israel would want a handsome, strong king that is head and shoulders taller then the rest. But the lesson is that God does not look at the outside of the person; rather, He looks on the inside. God was not pleased with King Saul (Shaul) because of a character flaw, where as David was a man after God's own heart, even though he was just a small shepherd boy.

Mordechai

Based on the book of Esther, during the Babylonian captivity of Judah, Mordechai rose up to courageously defend God's people. He was the son of Jair, of the tribe of Benyamin. Mordechai, Esther's uncle, was visible and at the king's court. When Hadassah lost her parents and became orphaned Mordechai adopted his cousin Hadassah (Esther from Aramaic) and raised her as his own.

> *Mordecai was sitting at the King's Gate. During those days while Mordecai was sitting at the King's Gate, Bigthan and Teresh, two eunuchs who guarded the king's entrance, became infuriated and planned to assassinate King Ahasuerus (Xerxes). When Mordecai learned of the plot, he reported it to Queen Esther, and she told the king on Mordecai's behalf. When the report was investigated and verified, both men were hanged on the gallows. This event was recorded in the historical record in the king's presence (**Esther 2:21-23 NIV**).*

Mordecai loved God with all his being and was willing to die for his people. He was the trusted gatekeeper of the Babylonian King Xerxes. Mordechai saved the Jews from total destruction and therefore does not fit the profile of a wolf.

Shaul of the New Testament

Prior to recognizing Yeshua as the Messiah, Shaul persecuted the followers of Yeshua. Notice his activity. In the morning, the wolf devours the prey. There are many metaphorical similarities to Shaul. He works alone as a hunter and killer of the believers or as one who approves the killing of Notzrim (converts). He hunts and then delivers his prey (Christians) in the evening to the Sanhedrin court.

> *When they had driven him [Stephen] out of the city, they began stoning him; and the witnesses laid aside their robes at the feet of a young man named Saul (**Acts 7:58 NASB**).*

> *On that day a great persecution broke out against the church in Jerusalem, and all except the apostles were scattered throughout Judea and Samaria. Godly men buried Stephen and mourned deeply for him. But Shaul began to destroy the church. Going from house to house, he dragged off both men and women and put them in prison (**Acts 8:1-3 NIV**).*

Meanwhile, Shaul was still breathing out murderous threats against the Lord's disciples. He went to the high priest and asked him for letters to the synagogues in Damascus, so that if he found any there who belonged to the Way, whether men or women, he might take them as prisoners to Yerushalaim (Acts 9:1-2 NIV).

After his eyes were opened to see Yeshua as the Messiah, the quality and fierceness Shaul inherited from his tribe was used to take the Good News to the world. The new sect was even apprehensive after Shaul's conversion. They were not sure if they could trust him, or if it was a trap to infiltrate among them and find out their secret meeting places. It took Shaul many travels, persecutions and hard work to persuade this new sect of people that he was one of them.

The misunderstanding and improper interpretation of Shaul's teachings caused confusion among the Christians Jewish converts resulting in arrests and ultimately death for many. These actions point to the possibility of Shaul fulfilling the role of the wolf from **Genesis 49**.

Shaul, the Keeper and Teacher of the Torah

Most Christians have the misconception that Shaul did not keep the laws of God given in the Old Testament. Yet he kept the laws concerning kosher eating, hygiene, Shabbat, the Holy Days, and was on the Sanhedrin court.

When Paul and his companions had passed through Amphipolis and Apollonia, they came to Thessalonica, where there was a Jewish synagogue. As was his custom, Paul went into the synagogue, and on three Sabbath days he reasoned with them from the Scriptures (Acts 17:1-2 NIV).

Every Sabbath he reasoned in the synagogue, trying to persuade Jews and Greeks (Acts 18:4 NIV).

*They arrived at Ephesus, where Paul left Priscilla and Aquila. He himself went into the synagogue and reasoned with the Jews (**Acts 18:19 NIV**).*

Shaul kept strict observance of the Torah to the day he died. If he truly was saying that the law had been abolished, then he was a hypocrite, keeping the Torah while teaching others not to. Careful scrutiny of the Scriptures shows he not only kept the law, he taught the Gentile believers to do the same. Consider the following verses and please pay attention to the emphasis given to certain words and phrases.

*For it is not those who hear the law who are **righteous** in God's sight, but it is those **who obey the law who will be declared righteous** (**Romans 2:13 NIV**).*

*So then, the law is holy, and the commandment is holy, righteous and good (**Romans 7:12 NIV**).*

*For in my inner being I delight in God's law; (**Romans 7:22 NIV**).*

The above Scripture very clearly shows Shaul's heart. He shares his adoration and zeal for the law of God. This is quite opposite of what the average Christian believes about Shaul. We don't have to take just Shaul's word concerning his observance of the Torah. New Testament Scripture shows that others recognized his obedience to the Torah.

*There was a great uproar, and some of the teachers of the law who were Pharisees stood up and argued vigorously. "We find nothing wrong with this man," they said. "What if a spirit or an angel has spoken to him?" (**Acts 23:9 NIV**)*

*They have been informed that you teach all the Jews who live among the Gentiles to turn away from Moses, [**away from the Torah**] telling them not to circumcise their children or*

*live according to our customs. What shall we do? They will
certainly hear that you have come, so do what we tell you.
There are four men with us who have made a vow. Take these
men, join in their purification rites and pay their expenses,
so that they can have their heads shaved. **Then everybody
will know there is no truth in these reports about you, but
that you yourself are living in obedience to the law (Acts
21:21-24 NIV).***

It is especially apparent in the Greek text that the rumors the
brothers heard about Shaul were not true. He was not teaching Jews
among the Gentiles to forsake Moshes, (Torah) circumcision, or
even the customs of the Jews. In **Acts 21:23-24** Shaul takes another
Nazarene vow with all the purification rites. The Nazarene vow
signified a desire to live a Kodesh (holy or separated) life as a Jew
before God. At this point he could have disavowed having anything
to do with the Torah by refusing to do as they asked, but he didn't.
He paid the expenses for all those who participated in the Nazarene
vow. He did so willingly in order to disprove the report that he was
living disobedient to the law. Shaul wasn't doing it to be deceptive
or to be a pleaser of men.

*Am I now trying to win the approval of men, or of God? Or
am I trying to please men? If I were still trying to please men,
I would not be a servant of Christ (**Galatians 1:10 NIV**).*

*Paul looked straight at the Sanhedrin and said, "My brothers,
I have fulfilled my duty to God in all good conscience to this
day (**Acts 23:1 NIV**).*

*Then Paul, knowing that some of them were Sadducees
and the others Pharisees, called out in the Sanhedrin, "My
brothers, I am a Pharisee, descended from Pharisees. I stand
on trial because of the hope of the resurrection of the dead"
(**Acts 23:6 NIV**).*

In **Acts 23:1**, Shaul calls the men in the Sanhedrin his brothers. He said he fulfilled his duty for God, which is another way of saying that he obeyed the law. In **Acts 23:6**, he said, "I am a Pharisee," not was a Pharisee. The other Perushim (Pharisees) didn't dispute Shaul's statement. They accepted him as being a Parush. At this point Shaul had been a believer in Yeshua for over twenty years and was still considered a Parush. Shaul's walk in the Torah, in the law, never changed because of Yeshua or His sacrifice. During this same period, he wrote the letter to the Romans and some of the other epistles.

Think about that, when you read those books. To correctly interpret Shaul, you must recognize that he was a Torah observant Jew, teaching others to observe the law as he did. If you interpret his writings as abolishing the law, then he would have to be some kind of schizophrenic, liar, or have multiple personalities. In **Acts 23:9**, the Perushim could find no fault with him.

> *Then Paul made his defense: "I have done nothing wrong against the Jewish law or against the temple or against Caesar" (Acts 25:8 NIV).*

> *Three days later he called together the local Jewish leaders. When they had assembled, Paul said to them: "My brothers, although I have done nothing against our people or against the customs of our ancestors, I was arrested in Jerusalem and handed over to the Romans" (Acts 28:17 NIV).*

In Shaul's defense before Festus in **Acts 25:8**, he said he observed the Torah. If Shaul was lying, we need to rip out some pages from the Bible. In **Acts 28:17** we find that Shaul did nothing against the customs of the Jews, which involves much more than the written Torah. Shaul did not give up being a Torah observant Jew to become a believer in Yeshua; He loved his Jewishness and was proud of it. He did not start a new religion. Believers in Yeshua remained a sect of Judaism for over one hundred years thanks to zealous students of the Torah like Rabbi Shaul. His life was dedicated to spreading the good news to both Jew and Gentile. May we all have the strength and zealousness of Rabbi Shaul. We give credit and validity to the Shaliach (apostle) Shaul both in the eyes of the Jews and in the eyes of many Gentiles. He is to be greatly esteemed, but never greater than Yeshua Ha'Mashiach.

Yeshua Fulfills Prophecy Concerning the Tribe of Ben 'Yamin

- **Yeshua took** on the sins of the world and became Ben Oni, (Son of my Sorrow).
- Yaakov's beloved wife Rachel in Hebrew means "sacrificial lamb". **Yeshua** became the Sacrificial Lamb for the sins of the world.
- After Rachel died, Yaakov, Ben'Oni's father changed his name to Ben 'Yamin (Son of my right hand). After **Yeshua** was resurrected He became the Son of God's right hand.
- Moshe, the personification of Yeshua raised Havoc to release his brothers, Israel from Egypt. **Yeshua** raised Havoc to release His brothers from the prison of sin.
- Shaul had the quality and fierceness of his tribe to take the Good News to the world. **Yeshua** is the fierce lion of the tribe of Yehudah.
- **Yeshua's** mission on the earth was short lived, only three and a half years. When He returns, He is returning as the King from the tribe of Yehudah. He will roar as the lion and will reign for a thousand years.
- **Yeshua** took upon Himself the sins of Ben 'YAmin and the sins of the world and became abhorrent to God. He was cut off from the living. On the third day, God raised His Son to sit at His right hand, thus becoming THE Ben 'Yamin, Son of God's right hand.

THE PHARISEES UNVEILED

*They have known me for a long time and can testify, if they are willing, that according to the strictest sect of our religion, I lived as a Pharisee (**Acts 26:5 NIV**).*

S haul was a Parush (Pharisee) and he was heavily influenced by his position with the Perushim (Pharisees). His upbringing in that sect molded and defined him. Yeshua the Messiah learned from and had much to say about the Perushim. Let's examine their primary functions, their role in the religious life and temple, and the extent of their authority and power. Although Yeshua the Messiah often castigated the Perushim for their arrogance, love of ceremony, hypocrisy and wickedness, he also had good things to say concerning them:

*Saying, "The scribes and the Pharisees sit in Moses' seat: All therefore whatsoever they bid you observe, that observe and do. . . (**Matthew 23:2-3 KJV**).*

Yeshua did not uphold the authority of Tzadikim (Sadducees) as he did with the Perushim. In fact Yeshua in no uncertain terms criticized them for their lack of knowledge of the Scripture and for denying the power of God and the resurrection of the dead.

*The same day came to him the Sadducees, which say that there is no resurrection, and asked him, Saying, Master, Moses said, If a man die, having no children, his brother shall marry his wife, and raise up seed unto his brother. Now there were with us seven brethren: and the first, when he had married a wife, deceased, and, having no issue, left his wife unto his brother: Likewise the second also, and the third, unto the seventh. And last of all the woman died also. Therefore in the resurrection whose wife shall she be of the seven? For they all had her. Yeshua answered and said unto them, Ye do err, not knowing the Scriptures, nor the power of God (**Matthew 22:23-29 KJV**).*

Yeshua upheld the Perushim authority, because they were knowledgeable and precise in their methodologies in teaching and exhorting the Torah. They were experts in using the entire Tanakh to explain it, using the verses contained within. They used oral traditions to bolster their teachings and arguments.

The Perushim established respect and authority because of their understanding and application of the Torah. Shaul is of this caliber of men. He makes his points by using and quoting Scripture, as did all Perushim. He is using the writings and the Scriptures that some in the Christian community say have been eradicated via Yeshua's sacrifice. Yeshua used the same teaching style the Perushim taught him. The Perushim acknowledged Yeshua's position and authority as a teacher. Depending on the translation you are reading, you will see he was regarded as master, teacher, or rabbi.

*Then certain of the scribes answering said, "Master (Rabbi) thou hast well said." And after that they durst not ask him any question at all (**Luke 20:39-40 KJV**).*

One of the teachers of the law came and heard them debating. Noticing that Jesus had given them a good answer, he asked him, "Of all the commandments, which is the most important?" "The most important one," answered Jesus, "is this: 'Hear, O Israel: The Lord our God, the Lord is one.

> *Love the Lord your God with all your heart and with all your*
> *soul and with all your mind and with all your strength.' The*
> *second is this: 'Love your neighbor as yourself.' There is no*
> *commandment greater than these." "Well said, teacher," the*
> *man replied. "You are right in saying that God is one and*
> *there is no other but him. To love him with all your heart,*
> *with all your understanding and with all your strength, and*
> *to love your neighbor as yourself is more important than all*
> *burnt offerings and sacrifices" (**Mark 12:28-33 NIV**).*

Not only did Yeshua do that which was in accordance with the law and the customs of his people, He did that which was in accordance to the customs of the teacher (Perushim) of his day.

> *And he came to Nazareth, where he had been brought up:*
> *and, as his custom was, he went into the synagogue on the*
> *Sabbath day, and stood up for to read (**Luke 4:16 KJV**).*

Yeshua's contempt of the Perushim was not intended to overthrow their authority. Even though that was the fear of the leadership, it was not His intent. This would have only undermined His authority.

The debt that true believers owe to the Perushim is substantial. Even though many of them became hypocrites and kept adding to the law in order to maintain power, they alone preserved the laws of God, the Torah. They preserved the unwritten laws that govern the calendar—the temple rituals, sacrifices and oral traditions that allow us to better understand the Torah today.

Consider the kind of men the Perushim were, especially in context of whether or not Shaul was actually teaching the abolishment of the law or adherence to the law. The Perushim observed the Torah and they were the teachers and judges of all things concerning the Torah. At the time of Yeshua the Pharisees were in great power. No one argued with them or confronted them.

> *Then stood there up one in the council, a Pharisee, named*
> *Gamliel, a doctor of the law, had in reputation among all*

*the people, and commanded to put the apostles forth a little space; And said unto them, Ye men of Israel, take heed to yourselves what ye intend to do as touching these men. For before these days rose up Theudas, boasting himself to be somebody; to whom a number of men, about four hundred, joined themselves: who was slain; and all, as many as obeyed him, were scattered, and brought to naught. After this man rose up Judas of Galilee in the days of the taxing, and drew away much people after him: he also perished and all, even as many as obeyed him, were dispersed. And now I say unto you, Refrain from these men, and let them alone: for if this counsel or this work be of men, it will come to naught: But if it be of God, ye cannot overthrow it; lest haply ye be found even to fight against God. And to him they agreed: and when they had called the apostles, and beaten them, they commanded that they should not speak in the name of Jesus, and let them go (**Acts 5:34-40 KJV**).*

Notice the influence Gamliel carried to sway the Tzadikim (Sadducees) and secure the release of the apostles. His credentials are impeccable as a Parush—and no doubt very powerful:

*I am verily a man which am a Jew, born in Tarsus, a city in Cilicia, yet **brought up in this city at the feet of Gamliel, and taught according to the perfect manner of the law of the fathers**, and was zealous toward God, as ye all are this day (**Acts 22:3 KJV**).*

*But when Paul perceived that the one part were Sadducees, and the other Pharisees, he cried out in the council, Men and brethren, I am a Pharisee, the son of a Pharisee: of the hope and resurrection of the dead I am called in question. And when he had so said, there arose a dissension between the Pharisees and the Sadducees: and the multitude was divided. For the Sadducees say that there is no resurrection, neither angel, nor spirit: but the Pharisees confess both (**Acts 23:6-8 KJV**).*

59

Shaul, in his defense before the Jews, emphasizes his connection to Gamliel. He wasn't merely making some declaration of faith. He was availing himself to the political power of the Perushim over the Tzadikim to procure his freedom.

Outside of the Bible, the best source of information about the Perushim is found in the writings of Yoseph Levy (Flavius Josephus). Not only was Yoseph a historian and general, he was also a Levite and Parush from the priestly order. In this light, his writings originate from the time the Perushim were at their height of power and influence. His writings give us a firsthand account of daily life after the revolt against Rome.

Josephus tells us that the Perushim exacted their observances and understanding of the law:

> "by succession from their fathers, which are not written in the laws of Moses . . . and concerning these things it is that great disputes and differences have arisen among them, while the Sadducees are able to persuade none but the rich, and have not the populace obsequious to them, but the Pharisees have the multitude on their side" (**Josephus Flavius,** *Antiquities of the Jews*, **Book 13, Chapter 10**).

The Sadducees rejected the unwritten tradition, which allowed the Perushim to accurately interpret and teach the Torah. The multitudes favored the Perushim, thus allowing them political power over those who disagree with them.

Josephus records the Perushim were scholarly and exacting with the laws of God. They were kind toward one another and the community at large. He hails them as the most accurate interpreters and unrivaled experts of the law.

> But then as to the two other orders at first mentioned, the **Pharisees are those who are esteemed most skillful in the exact explication of their laws,** and introduce the first sect. These ascribe all to fate [or providence], and to God, and yet allow, that to act what is right, or the contrary, is principally in the power of men, although fate does co-operate in every

action. They say that all souls are incorruptible, but that the souls of good men only are removed into other bodies, - but that the souls of bad men are subject to eternal punishment. But the Sadducees are those that compose the second order, and take away fate entirely, and suppose that God is not concerned in our doing or not doing what is evil; and they say, that to act what is good, or what is evil, is at men's own choice, and that the one or the other belongs so to every one, that they may act as they please. They also take away the belief of the immortal duration of the soul, and the punishments and rewards in Hades. **Moreover, the Pharisees are friendly to one another, and are for the exercise of concord, and regard for the public;** but the behavior of the Sadducees one towards another is in some degree wild, and their conversation with those that are of their own party is as barbarous as if they were strangers to them. And this is what I had to say concerning the philosophic sects among the Jews **(Josephus Flavius,** *War of the Jews***, Book II, chapter 8 Section 14).**

The writings of Josephus not only show the deep involvement of the Perushim in civil duties and the temple, but they wielded a vast amount of power over the people and religious life during the time of Yeshua. He paints them in a pleasing light with regards to their adherence and abilities to teach and judge according to the Torah. It was the Perushim that Israel consulted for leadership in all matters.

When you consider the involvement Shaul had with the Perushim, why are today's churches so quick to abandon the laws of God he lived by and use his writings as their justification? There is an incredible divide between who Shaul was, what he taught and how some churches portray Shaul and his writings today.

ONE OF MANY

*I planted the seed, Apollos watered it, but God has been
making it grow. So neither the one who plants nor the one
who waters is anything, but only God, who makes things
grow (**1 Corinthians 3:6-7 NIV**).*

*P*aul was one of many who shared the Gospel and preached
Yeshua. He is sometimes given undo credit for many things he
never did. Many have credited the establishment of the synagogue
in Rome and some synagogues in Africa and Asia Minor to Shaul,
however the Scripture reveals a different story. From the book of
Acts 2:10-11 we find Jews came from all over to attend the Feast of
Shavuot (Pentecost). They came in obedience to the Torah and not
because of Shaul's influence.

It is commanded for Jews to come to Jerusalem three times a
year to bring their offerings and tithes to the temple, so the knowledge of God and His Word were known around the world. Shaul was
commissioned to go and preach the message of salvation long after
this pilgrimage was established.

*Phrygia and Pamphylia, Egypt and the parts of Libya near
Cyrene; visitors from Rome   (both Jews and converts to
Judaism); Cretans and Arabs—we hear them declaring the
wonders of God in our own tongues! (**Acts 2:10-11 NIV**)*

*I do not want you to be unaware, brothers, that I planned many times to come to you (but have been prevented from doing so until now) in order that I might have a harvest among you, just as I have had among the other Gentiles. I am obligated both to Greeks [Gentiles] and non-Greeks [Jews], both to the wise [Torah students] and the foolish [the ignorant of Torah]. That is why I am so eager to preach the gospel also to you who are at Rome. I am not ashamed of the gospel, because it is the power of God for the salvation of everyone who believes: first for the Jew, then for the Gentile (**Romans 1:13-16 NIV**).*

*It has always been my ambition to preach the gospel where Christ was not known, so that I would not be building on someone else's foundation (**Romans 15:20 NIV**).*

*Neither do we go beyond our limits by boasting of work done by others. Our hope is that, as your faith continues to grow, our area of activity among you will greatly expand, so that we can preach the gospel in the regions beyond you. For we do not want to boast about work already done in another man's territory (**2 Corinthians 10:15-16 NIV**).*

We see from the above Scriptures that **Shaul is not teaching anything new.** He is teaching exactly what the other workers of Yeshua taught who preceded him in those regions. Shaul knows he is not the only apostle continuing the work of Yeshua. He is careful not to overshadow the labor done by other workers of Yeshua. People get attached to their teachers in style and in personality, but if the foundation of their teaching is the same, none should be exalted above the other.

THE HEAVENLY ORDER

*T*here is an order appointed in the universe that started in heaven. Consider that everything flows from the Father through His Son Yeshua (who only does the will of His Father), then to angels and then to men. Men were given authority over the earth.

> *What advantage, then, is there in being a Jew, or what value is there in circumcision? Much in every way! First of all, they have been entrusted with the very words of God (**Romans 3:1-2 NIV**).*

Cornelius, a Roman centurion desiring to know the Jewish God sought council from the Pharisees in Jerusalem. He asked them, "We have many gods in Rome but they are all visible and all of them were made by our craftsman, but you worship an invisible God, and you are willing to die for this invisible God. As a soldier I understand loyalty and commitment. I salute you for your love and sacrifice for your God. I want to know this God."

The rabbis told him the answer to his quest could only be achieved through prayer and fasting and taught him how to pray and fast according to the law. Cornelius prayed and fasted as he was taught; on the third day an angel from heaven appeared to him. By this time Cornelius was neither afraid nor surprised from the heavenly being, as he listened to the angel's instruction.

Cornelius did not demand that the angel teach him the truth. Men on earth know more about God's truth than an angel coming from heaven from the presence of Adonai, yet Cornelius submitted himself to the command of the angel because he understood the delegation of authority. The angel sent Cornelius to seek a man whose name was Shimon (Peter) who was given the keys to the kingdom of God on earth.

The keys to the kingdom meant the keys to understanding the principles of Torah. The keys refer to power and authority to bind, to loosen and to expound the Scriptures. Shimon spent the entire three and a half years with Yeshua and many times, the Master Yeshua lodged in Peter's house. No doubt many secrets were revealed to him by the Master in order for Yeshua to entrust him with the keys to the kingdom. Cornelius was instructed to go to the commanding officer in God's kingdom, Shimon, not Shaul, not Yochanan the beloved—not even Yeshua's brother Ya'acov (James). If we are to take sides on this issue who would you follow?

A WARNING FROM PETER

S himon (Peter or Petros, which means "rock" in Greek) Peter is the only man on earth entrusted with the keys to the kingdom given to him by Yeshua himself.

> *And I tell you that you are Peter, and on this rock I will build my church, and the gates of Hades will not overcome it. I will give you the keys of the kingdom of heaven; whatever you bind on earth will be bound in heaven, and whatever you loose on earth will be loosed in heaven (**Matthew 16:18-19 NIV**).*

Because of this, Shimon (Peter) speaks with authority that supersedes that of Shaul's. Even with the authority that Shimon (Peter) had from Yeshua, Shimon (Peter) did not change or void God's laws. Shimon says of Shaul:

> *He writes the same way in all his letters, speaking in them of these matters. His letters contain some things that are **hard to understand**, which **ignorant and unstable** people distort, as they do the other Scriptures, to their own destruction (**2 Peter 3:16 NIV**).*

No other man in the Bible warns us about another man's writings the way Shimon did about some of Shaul's work. The debate about whether or not the law was abolished was going on during Shaul's time and continues to this day. Shimon's warning is for all of us. He is telling us to keep our eyes on the Torah and do what it says, just as Yeshua did before His death and resurrection.

SHAUL AND THE LAW

*T*he issues surrounding Shaul's message did not start in the twentieth century. It started during Shaul's lifetime and has continued ever since. The problem people have with what Shaul is saying is not really with what he is saying, it is more with what they are taught to think he is saying. Christianity has done a great disservice to Shaul's message.

Shaul does not dismiss obedience to the law. He dismisses obedience without faith in Yeshua the Mashiach who was crucified for our sins. Shaul consistently teaches salvation through faith. He does not teach that the Law of Moshe is abolished, although he does dismiss traditions, like not eating with Gentiles that were additions not found in the Torah:

> . . .*know that a man is not justified by observing the law, but by faith in Yeshua Ha'Mashiach. So we, too, have put our faith in Mashiach Yeshua that we may be justified by faith in Christ and not by observing the law, because by observing the law no one will be justified. "If, while we seek to be justified in Christ, it becomes evident that we ourselves are sinners, does that mean that Christ promotes sin?* **Absolutely not!** *(***God forbid! KJV***) If I rebuild what I destroyed, I prove that I am a lawbreaker. For through the law I died to the law so that I might live for God. I have been crucified with Christ*

and I no longer live, but Christ lives in me. The life I live in the body, I live by faith in the Son of God, who loved me and gave himself for me. I do not set aside the grace of God, for if righteousness could be gained through the law, Christ died for nothing! **(Galatians 2:16-3:1 NIV)**

Many teach that faith was introduced to us by Shaul. We have plenty of evidence both in the Old and New Testament where men expressed faith. Cain and Able first expressed faith when he sacrificed to Adonai. Noah proclaimed his faith in Adonai by building a boat that took him one hundred years. By faith, Abraham left his family at the order of Adonai and offered his only son as a sacrifice, who God spared. In the New Testament, Yeshua, the Son of God comes to this earth with total obedience through faith in His Father's ability to resurrect and restore Him back to His rightful place.

Shaul states that a person is not justified by the works of the law, but through faith in Yeshua. Shaul is reminding his audience that before any act can take place in obedience to God, one must first believe. In Hebrew the root word comes from AMEN and is an action much like a commitment to act on a promissory note. Shaul states that if we were found to be sinners (lawbreakers) it would mean that Yeshua is a minister of sin. We know this is not true. Shaul agrees, stating in **Galatians 2:17,** *"God forbid!"* Therefore, it is plain that we are not to be found as lawbreakers, or breaking the law.

You foolish Galatians! Who has bewitched you? Before your very eyes Jesus Christ was clearly portrayed as crucified. I would like to learn just one thing from you: Did you receive the Spirit by observing the law, or by believing what you heard? **(Galatians 3:1-2 NIV)**

Shaul asks the Galatians who bewitched them into thinking they can earn their salvation by the law. He brings the point home by following up with this question, *"Did you receive the Spirit by observing the law, or by believing what you heard?"* Obviously they received the spirit (knowledge) by hearing and having faith in Yeshua. Faith comes by hearing, but hearing what? Hearing the Word of Torah.

THE WORD OF TORAH

*Y*aakov (James), who was the brother of Yeshua, continued to teach the law weekly in the synagogues at the council in Jerusalem. The law was read on Shabbat so the people learned to obey.

> *For Moses has been preached in every city from the earliest times and is read in the synagogues on every Sabbath (**Acts 15:21 NIV**).*

The challenge Shaul had with the Jewish people was convincing them that the initial law given to Adam in the Garden brought the ability for man to make a choice whether to obey God or not. Without a law given, there can be no breaking of the law. When Adam disobeyed, sin entered and it brought a curse to all humanity. Yeshua Himself sacrificed the first kosher animal and covered Adam, which showed an outward expression portraying inward repentance. Sin demanded life, since life is in the blood; kosher animals were chosen to substitute for the life of the sinner.

This was a visual picture of how God would send the perfect Lamb of God who would be the ultimate sacrifice for the sins of the world fulfilling the need for all animal sacrifices. A believer in Yeshua who continues with animal sacrifices after the death of Yeshua denies His ultimate sacrifice making it of no avail. Therefore if one continues to sacrifice animals, they are denying the reason

Yeshua came, which was to put an end to ALL blood sacrifices by becoming a sacrifice for all who believe in Him,

> *All who rely on observing the law are under a curse, (**It should be said they are under obligation-not curse**) for it is written: "Cursed is everyone who does not continue to do everything written in the Book of the Law." Clearly no one is justified before God by the law, because, "The righteous will live by faith." The law is not based on faith; on the contrary, "The man who does these things will live by them." Christ redeemed us from the curse [**obligation**] of the law by becoming a curse for us, for it is written: "Cursed is everyone who is hung on a tree" (**Galatians 3:10-13 NIV**).*

> *Cursed is anyone who does not uphold the words of this law by carrying them out. Then all the people shall say, "Amen!" (**Deuteronomy 27:26 NIV**)*

That is Shaul's consistent struggle. He contrasts obedience without faith and faith with obedience. Making the contrast that one can be obedient to the law without believing and not be "saved" (using church terminology). He also consistently points out that if one has faith, the law will be learned, observed and followed resulting in salvation.

> *For if the inheritance depends on the law, then it no longer depends on a promise; but God in his grace gave it to Abraham through a promise. What, then, was the purpose of the law? It was added because of transgressions until the Seed to whom the promise referred had come. The law was put into effect through angels by a mediator (**Galatians 3:18-19 NIV**).*

Avraham showed his faith by his obedience. It is intellectually dishonest or lazy for people to use this verse to argue against the law. Shaul states that the law was added because of transgressions ordained by an angel (messenger). In my opinion **this messenger or angel is Moshe** (messenger from Strong's 4397).

> *At that time I stood between the LORD and you to declare to you the word of the LORD, because you were afraid of the fire and did not go up the mountain. And he said. . . (**Deuteronomy 5:5 NIV**).*

> *. . . to Moses, "Speak to us yourself and we will listen. But do not have God speak to us or we will die" (**Exodus 20:19 NIV**).*

> *But before faith came, we were kept under the law, shut up unto the faith which should afterwards be revealed (**Galatians 3:23 KJV**).*

Shaul states that we are kept under the law. This word *kept* is the Greek word *phrouros* meaning "guarded." This word is more similar to the Hebrew word *shamar* meaning "to keep, guard, watch or preserve." Sadly, the churches put the word kept in a negative light when in context it means the law was given to protect us. Again, their ignorance shows itself.

> *So the law was put in charge to lead us to Christ that we might be justified by faith. Now that faith has come, we are no longer under the supervision of the law (**Galatians 3:24-25 NIV**).*

From the above verse one might conclude that faith is new, that it appeared after Yeshua came on the scene. Faith has been here since the beginning of time. We see examples of faith in Genesis when Noah believed God by building a wooden ark. It took him one hundred years to build in spite of the fact that it had never rained on the earth. Using theses words in the above verse, ***now that faith has come, or has arrived,*** is speaking about the person of Yeshua. Now that HE, Yeshua, has arrived we no longer need sacrifice and no longer need a priest to supervise the legal aspect of the law.

The law is a tutor that can lead us to Yeshua, and as a result, our justification will be by our faith in Yeshua. He expands on this idea when He writes we are no longer under a tutor. Here Shaul emphasizes that the natural result of our faith will be our obedience. We need not be under the curse of the law (death) by disobedience or under a tutor (law) of sacrifices because the law (tutor) brings us to Yeshua. With Yeshua we will become observers of God's law naturally. How could we not? If disobeying the law brought separation between men and God, then it stands to reason that redemption will be achieved through obedience to the lawgiver.

> *For Christ is the end of the law for righteousness to every one that believeth (**Romans 10:4 KJV**).*

Shaul continues this idea that obedience without faith will not bring salvation. It is only by obedience with and through faithfulness that one will be found worthy. Yeshua is the end of righteousness through the law. Shaul illustrates that blind obedience is not enough. You must also have faith in Yeshua Mashiach, the Son of the living God and His sacrifice for our sins:

> *But what saith it? The word is nigh thee, even in thy mouth, and in thy heart: that is, the word of faith, which we preach. . . (**Romans 10:8 KJV**).*

> *But the word is very nigh unto thee, in thy mouth, and in thy heart, that thou mayest do it (**Deuteronomy 30:14 KJV**).*

If the Word is in our hearts and in our mouth, as a result we will be obedient. Shaul prescribes that the law (Torah) should be ingrained in our hearts. When mastering anything important, it takes time and practice to make our responses automatic. In martial arts, the student practices until he comes to a point where he does not need to continually ask the teacher if his moves are correct. When we spend our life studying the Torah, our response to turn from sin becomes automatic, not one of needing to continually ask a preacher or rabbi, "Is this sin?" Yeshua response to Satan when tempted in the wilderness was, "***It is Written***". His response was automatic and immediate because of the years spent studying the Torah.

In none of these verses does Shaul teach contrary to the law. Instead, he upholds it in the same manner as Parush. He magnifies the law just as Yeshua did in the sermon on the Mount.

> *Ye have heard that it was said by them of old time, Thou shalt not commit adultery: But I say unto you, that whosoever looketh on a woman to lust after her hath committed adultery with her already in his heart. And if thy right eye offends thee, pluck it out, and cast it from thee: for it is profitable for thee that one of thy members should perish, and not that thy whole body should be cast into hell. And if thy right hand offend thee, cut it off, and cast it from thee: for it is profitable for thee that one of thy members should perish, and not that thy whole body should be cast into hell (**Matthew 5:27-30 KJV**).*

For people who truly believe Shaul's teachings are a dismissal of the law and people are saved only on the basis of faith regardless of their actions, let us consider the words of Yeshua in **Matthew 5: 27-30**. Yeshua states that sin is not simply an act only, but even in the thinking of our mind. According to these verses, sin went from the Law of Moshe with **an act of disobedience** against the law to Yeshua's deeper expansion of inward intent, that if a man looks at a woman with lust he has committed adultery. This was not a new idea from Yeshua. We find similar teachings in the Torah. The command not to make images (Tmunah or picture) applies to Yeshua's comment that sin originates in the mind. Envy or covetousness begins in the mind. Wanting something you do not posses is coveting, which leads to all other outward sins—including adultery.

With this in mind, do you still think that Shaul had the power and authority to change the law of Yeshua? Do you still believe that Rabbi Shaul would defy his rabbi's teachings? In **Galatians 1:8-9** Shaul warns that if a false prophet or a dreamer of dreams or even an angel of light were to appear and teach anything contrary to Scripture, we are not to follow.

> *But though we, or an angel (Messenger) from heaven, preach any other gospel unto you than that which we have preached unto you, let him be accursed. As we said before, so say I now again, if any man preach any other gospel unto you than that ye have received, let him be accursed (**Galatians 1:8-9 KJV**).*

Shaul was pointing to himself and anyone else who might be construed as teaching contrary to the law. His warnings mirror the warning given by God in Deuteronomy and Ezekiel and the warning of Yeshua that many false messiahs would appear to deceive the every elect.

It does not make any sense to castigate Shaul as a denier of the Torah when that is all he quoted and taught. He even asked for his books and parchments to be brought to him, referring to his winter coat, the Torah and the prophets:

> *The cloke that I left at Troas with Carpus, when thou comest, bring with thee, and the books [prophets], but especially the parchments [**the Torah**] (**2 Timothy 4:13 KJV**).*

Rabbis could not teach an audience unless they had the Torah scroll. Shaul was ready to hunker in for the winter and have people come to him to study the Torah.

Shaul's consistent teaching is that all men fall short on their own and that once they believe, they should no longer live in sin, but strive for righteousness. He understands and teaches that one can attain the ability to not sin or at least give all of their effort not to sin. The breaking of God's law is sin—therefore a person who keeps God's law by his acceptance of Yeshua's sacrifice for their sin will change from desires of sin to desires of pleasing his Heavenly Father by doing what He commands.

Shaul forewarned us about these days when people would openly separate themselves from the laws of Adonai:

Don't let anyone deceive you in any way, for that day will not come until the rebellion occurs and the man of lawlessness is revealed, the man doomed to destruction. He will oppose and will exalt himself over everything that is called God or is worshiped, so that he sets himself up in God's temple, proclaiming himself to be God. Don't you remember that when I was with you I used to tell you these things? And now you know what is holding him back, so that he may be revealed at the proper time. **For the secret power of lawlessness is already at work;** *but the one who now holds it back will continue to do so till he is taken out of the way. And then the lawless one will be revealed, whom the Lord Yeshua will overthrow with the breath of his mouth and destroy by the splendor of his coming. The coming of the lawless one will be in accordance with the work of Satan displayed in all kinds of counterfeit miracles, signs and wonders, and in every sort of evil that deceives those who are perishing.* **They perish because they refused to love the truth and so be saved (2 Thessalonians 2:3-10 NIV).**

For such men are false apostles, deceitful workmen, masquerading as apostles of Christ. *And no wonder, for Satan himself masquerades as an angel of light.* **It is not surprising, then, if his servants masquerade as servants of righteousness.** *Their end will be what their actions deserve* **(2 Corinthians 11:13-15 NIV).**

Re-read **2 Thessalonians 2:10**, *"They perish because they refused to love the truth and so be saved."* The godless perished because they refused the truth (Torah), which would allow them to be saved (acquire salvation). Shaul speaks of the false apostles perpetuating this teaching.

This makes perfect sense when you consider the Hebrew word for Torah means *teacher* or *pointed instruction* and the Hebrew word for Yeshua means *salvation*. The Torah is Adonai's instructions to teach mankind how to live righteously and acquire salvation through Yeshua. To think that contradicts **Isaiah 2:3** this shows otherwise.

*Many peoples will come and say, "Come, let us go up to the mountain of the LORD, to the house of the God of Jacob. **He will teach us his ways, so that we may walk in his paths." The law will go out from Zion, the word of the LORD from Jerusalem (Isaiah 2:3 NIV).***

This prophecy shows a time when both Jew and Gentile will be learning the Torah from Yeshua. If Yeshua is to rule the earth for a thousand years, He will rule with the one eternal law—the Torah.

*Repent, then, and turn to God, so that your sins may be wiped out, that times of refreshing may come from the Lord, and that he may send the Christ, who has been appointed for you—even Yeshua. **He must remain in heaven until the time comes for God to restore everything,** as he promised long ago through his holy prophets. For Moses said, **"The Lord your God will raise up for you a prophet like me from among your own people; you must listen to everything he tells you. Anyone who does not listen to him will be completely cut off from among his people."** "Indeed, all the prophets from Samuel on, as many as have spoken, have foretold these days. And you are heirs of the prophets and of the covenant God made with your fathers. He said to Abraham, 'Through your offspring all peoples on earth will be blessed.' When God raised up his servant, **he sent him first to you to bless you by turning each of you from your wicked ways"** (Acts 3:19-26 NIV).*

There is so much hidden in these few verses from Shaul. He speaks of a time Yeshua will return to restore everything broken by man—specifically the Torah. He reiterates the prophecy of Moshe stating that Yeshua is the prophet everyone should obey. Yeshua said, *"If you love me, keep my commandments."* Moshe didn't say anything about obeying Shaul. To avoid being cut off from God's people, we should obey Yeshua who never once spoke of the passing of the law.

In addition to all your other detestable practices, you brought foreigners uncircumcised in heart and flesh into my sanctuary, desecrating my temple while you offered me food, fat and blood, and you broke my covenant. Instead of carrying out your duty in regard to my holy things, you put others in charge of my sanctuary. This is what the Sovereign LORD says: **No foreigner uncircumcised in heart and flesh is to enter my sanctuary, not even the foreigners who live among the Israelites (Ezekiel 44:7-9 NIV).**

What is the basis upon which so many believe it is acceptable to disregard God's law?

Surely the day is coming; it will burn like a furnace. All the arrogant and every evildoer will be stubble, and that day that is coming will set them on fire," says the LORD Almighty. "Not a root or a branch will be left to them. But for you who revere my name, the sun of righteousness will rise with healing in its wings. And you will go out and leap like calves released from the stall. Then you will trample down the wicked; they will be ashes under the soles of your feet on the day when I do these things," says the LORD Almighty. "Remember the law of my servant Moses, the decrees and laws I gave him at Horeb for all Israel" **(Malachi 4:1-4 NIV).**

There is no place in the Tanakh (Old Testament) that will validate their claims. There is no evidence in the Gospels that the law was or would be done away with.

Whoever has my commands and keeps them is the one who loves me. The one who loves me will be loved by my Father, and I too will love them and show myself to them. Whoever has my commands and keeps them is the one who loves me. The one who loves me will be loved by my Father, and I too will love them and show myself to them **(John 14:21 NIV).**

One cannot find proof in the books of James, Peter, John or Jude concerning the abolition of the law. Yet some Christians, professing to follow the example and teachings of Yeshua continue to teach that we no longer need to obey the Ten Commandments. They teach that the Ten Commandments are not binding upon the new covenant. So where do the Gentiles draw their conclusions? The answer, of course, is in selected sections of the apostle Shaul's writings. Yet the Scriptures of the other writers who were firsthand witnesses of Yeshua confirm that the Torah is to be obeyed by all.

YESHUA VERSUS SHAUL

*D*id Shaul oppose the teachings of Yeshua, or did he submit to Yeshua's teaching? To start answering that question, we must learn about Yeshua and Shaul's teachings. Shaul claims he was a Parush (Pharisee) who studied at the feet of Gamliel. Hillel was the grandfather of Gamliel and taught one of the two major schools of thought in his day. The school of Hillel influenced Yeshua and most of His parables reflect that school of thought. Yet there were some things Yeshua spoke about that can be directly tied to the school of Shammai.

This is apparent when a Parush (lawyer) questioned Yeshua as to which commandment He viewed as the most important. Yeshua's response as given in the Gospels of Mark, Matthew and Luke was:

> *Love the Lord your God with all your heart and with all your soul and with all your mind. This is the first and greatest commandment. And the second is like it: Love your neighbor as yourself. All the Law and the Prophets hang on these two commandments (**Mark 12:28-34; Matthew 22:34-40; Luke 10:25-28**).*

Yeshua was quoting **the Torah:**

*Hear, O Israel: The LORD our God, the LORD is one. Love the LORD your God with all your heart and with all your soul and with all your strength (**Deuteronomy 6:4-5 NIV**).*

*Do not seek revenge or bear a grudge against one of your people, but love your neighbor as yourself. I am the LORD (**Leviticus 19:18 NIV**).*

Deuteronomy 6:4 contains the central prayer known to Jews as the Shema. It is considered the foundation of Jewish prayer and belief. Yeshua uses the foundation of Jewish prayer and belief to answer the question. The Shema is a confession of who God is based on **Deuteronomy 6:4.** From the Shema, Yeshua delivers the first and second most important commandments upon which all the Torah is based.

Yeshua's answer about loving God and one's neighbor was a well-known refrain of the Parush. Loving your neighbor is required in order to be able to love God. If you cannot love the person in front of you, the one you see, how can you say you love God whom you cannot see? Rabbi Akiva considered loving your neighbor as the major principle of the Torah (**JT Nedarim 9:4**). This is a teaching that Rabbi Hillel endorsed. He said, "What is hateful to yourself do not do to another, that is the whole law, the rest is commentary" (**BT Shab. 31a**). Yeshua echoed Rabbi Hillel when he said, *"In everything do to others as you would have them do to you. . .for this is the law and the prophets"* (**Matthew 7:12**).

Hillel taught not to judge your fellow man until you yourself come into his place or walk in his shoes (**M. Avot 2:5**). Yeshua gives a similar saying when he said not to judge and you will not be judged (**Luke 6:37**). Both of these sayings are based on the commandment to love your neighbor as yourself.

*Do not judge, and you will not be judged. Do not condemn, and you will not be condemned. Forgive, and you will be forgiven (**Luke 6:37 NIV**).*

*Jesus answered, "I am the way and the truth and the life. No one comes to the Father except through me" (**John 14:6 NIV**).*

In **John 14:6,** Yeshua said that He was the way, which is the Torah the rabbis use a silver hand with an index finger extended out called the pointer to read the Torah so as not to touch the scroll. The pointer is Yeshua, pointing to us that the way is found in the Torah, which is Yeshua. This suggests that while Yeshua is the **way** people should follow, the Temple leaders also dictate the way. The way was determined by the leaders of that day and was called Halacha, (the Hebrew word *Halach*, Strong's 1980) which means, "to walk." Halacha means the way one *should* walk.

*The teachers of the law and the Pharisees sit in Moses' seat. **So you must obey them and do everything they tell you.** But do not do what they do, for they do not practice what they preach (**Matthew 23:2-3 NIV**).*

When Yeshua spoke of the Perushim sitting in the chair of Moses, He was simply saying that when they instruct you in the writings of Moshe. Listen to them and obey them. We see the influence of Halacha in the day Yeshua lived. The Halacha, which was the proper dictate and proper conduct, helped direct the people on how best to observe the commandments of Adonai.

*It hath been said, whosoever shall put away his wife, let him give her a writing of divorcement: But I say unto you, That whosoever shall put away his wife, saving for the cause of fornication, causeth her to commit adultery: and whoso-ever shall marry her that is divorced committeth adultery (**Matthew 5:31-32 KJV**).*

In Galilee, divorce was forbidden even though the Torah gave allowances for divorce. Yeshua was from Galilee and endorsed the Halacha. **Matthew 5:31-32** records his response to the divorce question. In other areas, the Galilean Halacha was less strict. In the dietary laws, fowl was the equivalent of fish; therefore it could be cooked with milk. The Jews of Judea considered fowl to be meat and thus restricted it from being cooked with milk or milk products.

Other areas where the influence of Halacha can be seen include healing on the Shabbat, or picking/crushing grain from the field. These issues were debated and challenged within the Gospels and the end resulted in determinations (Halacha) that were well within the range of keeping the Torah. None were considered to be an abandonment of Torah observance.

Let's examine a few samples of the synoptic teachings between Shaul and Yeshua.

Resurrection

Yeshua: *"For just as the Father raises the dead and gives them life, even so the Son also gives life to whom He wishes"* (***John 5:21 KJV***).

Shaul: *"For as in Adam all die, so also in Christ all shall be made alive"* (***1 Corinthians 15:22 NASB***).

Concern and Worry

Yeshua: *"For this reason I say to you, do not be worried about your life, as to what you shall eat, or what you shall drink; nor for your body, as to what you shall put on. Is not life more than food, and the body more than clothing?"* (***Matthew 6:25 NASB***)

Shaul: *"Be anxious for nothing, but in everything by prayer and supplication with thanksgiving let your requests be made known to God"* (***Philippians 4:6 NASB***).

Yeshua the Sacrifice

Yeshua: *"I am the good shepherd; the good shepherd lays down His life for the sheep"* (***John 10:11 KJV***).

Shaul: *". . .and walk in love, just as Christ also loved you, and gave Himself up for us, an offering and a sacrifice to God as a fragrant aroma"* (***Ephesians 5:2 KJV***).

Yeshua's Genealogy

"The LORD brought me forth as the first of his works, before his deeds of old; I was appointed from eternity, from the beginning, before the world began. When there were no oceans, I was given birth, when there were no springs abounding with water; before the mountains were settled in place, before the hills, I was given birth, before he made the earth or its fields or any of the dust of the world. I was there when he set the heavens in place, when he marked out the horizon on the face of the deep, when he established the clouds above and fixed securely the fountains of the deep, when he gave the sea its boundary so the waters would not overstep his command, and when he marked out the foundations of the earth. Then I was the craftsman at his side. I was filled with delight day after day, rejoicing always in his presence, rejoicing in his whole world and delighting in mankind. "Now then, my sons, listen to me; blessed are those who keep my ways. Listen to my instruction and be wise; do not ignore it. Blessed is the man who listens to me, watching daily at my doors, waiting at my doorway. 35 For whoever finds me finds life and receives favor from the LORD. But whoever fails to find me harms himself; all who hate me love death" (***Proverbs 8:22-36 NIV***).

God said to Moses, "I AM WHO I AM. This is what you are to say to the Israelites: I AM has sent me to you" (***Exodus 3:14 NIV***).

Yeshua: *"I tell you the truth," Yeshua answered, "before Abraham was born, I am!" (**John 8:58 NIV**)*

Shaul: *"For in Christ all the fullness of the Deity lives in bodily form" (**Colossians 2:9 NIV**).*

Shaul: *"Who, being in very nature God, did not consider equality with God something to be grasped, but made himself nothing, taking the very nature of a servant, being made in human likeness. And being found in appearance as a man, he humbled himself and became obedient to death—even death on a cross!" (**Philippians 2:6-8 NIV**)*

Forgiveness

Yeshua: *"For if you forgive others for their transgressions, your heavenly Father will also forgive you" (**Matthew 6:14 NASB**).*

Shaul: *"Be kind and compassionate to one another, forgiving each other, just as in Christ God forgave you" (**Ephesians 4:32 NIV**).*

Yeshua Is the Way

Yeshua: *"Yeshua said to him, 'I am the Way, and the Truth, and the Life; no one comes to the Father, but through Me'" (**John 14:6 KJV**).*

Shaul: *"For there is one God, and one mediator also between God and men, the man Yeshua Ha' Mashiach" (**1 Timothy 2:5 KJV**).*

Justification by Faith

Yeshua: *"Truly, truly, I say to you, he who hears My word, and believes Him who sent Me, has eternal life, and does not* *come into judgment, but has passed out of death into life"* (**John 5:24 NASB**).

Yeshua: *"To some who were confident of their own righteousness and looked down on everybody else, Jesus told this parable: "Two men went up to the temple to pray, one a Pharisee and the other a tax collector. The Pharisee stood up and prayed about himself: 'God, I thank you that I am not like other men, robbers, evildoers, adulterers or even like this tax collector. I fast twice a week and give a tenth of all I get.' "But the tax collector stood at a distance. He would not even look up to heaven, but beat his breast and said, 'God, have mercy on me, a sinner'"* (**Luke 18:9-13 NIV**).

Yeshua: *"For God so loved the world that he gave his one and only Son, that whoever believes in him shall not perish but have eternal life. For God did not send his Son into the world to condemn the world, but to save the world through him. Whoever believes in him is not condemned, but whoever does not believe stands condemned already because he has not believed in the name of God's one and only Son"* (**John 3:16-18 NIV**).

Shaul: *"Therefore having been justified by faith-fullness, we have peace with God through our Lord Yeshua Ha'Mashiach"* (**Romans 5:1 NASB**).

The Establishment Of the Law

Yeshua: *"Do not think that I came to abolish the Law or the prophets; I did not come to abolish, but to fulfill"* (**Matthew 5:17 NASB**).

Shaul: *"Do we then nullify the Law through faith? May it never be! On the contrary, we establish the law"* (**Romans 3:31 NASB**).

Shaul*: "What I mean is this: The law, introduced 430 years later, does not set aside the covenant previously established by God and thus do away with the promise" (**Galatians 3:17 NIV**).*

The Ten Commandments Simplified

Yeshua*: "You shall not commit murder; You shall not commit adultery; You shall not steal; You shall not bear false witness; Honor your father and mother; and You shall love your neighbor as yourself" (**Matthew 19:18-19 NASB**).*

Shaul*: "Owe nothing to anyone except to love one another; for he who loves his neighbor has fulfilled the law. For this, 'You shall not commit adultery, You shall not murder, You shall not steal, You shall not covet,' and if there is any other commandment, it is summed up in this saying, 'You shall love your neighbor as yourself.' Love does no wrong to a neighbor; love therefore is the fulfillment of the law" (**Romans 13:8-10 NASB**).*

Predestination

Yeshua*: "Not all men can accept this statement, but only those to whom it has been given" (**Matthew 19:11 KJV**).*

Yeshua*: "All that the Father gives Me shall come to Me, and the one who comes to Me I will certainly not cast out" (**John 6:37 NASB**).*

Yeshua*: "No one can come to Me, unless the Father who sent Me draws him; and I will raise him up on the last day" (**John 6:44 KJV**).*

Yeshua*: "For this reason I have said to you, that no one can come to Me, unless it has been granted him from the Father" (**John 6:65 KJV**).*

Shaul*: "He predestined us to adoption as sons through Yeshua to Himself, according to the kind intention of His will. . .also we have obtained an inheritance, having been predestined according to His purpose who works all things after the counsel of His will" (**Ephesians 1:5,11 KJV**).*

Predestination by no means signifies that we are puppets in the hands of our creator with no choice about our destiny. We were given free choice to chose to serve God or to serve the enemy, otherwise the death of Yeshua is to no avail. God being omnipotent (all knowing) knows our thoughts; He also knows what our choice will be before we do, just as a person knows in advance that if he was to strike a match on gasoline it will catch on fire, he knows it before he strikes the match. This does not mean he has somehow forced it to catch fire or had any influence on the fuel, he just knows that fuel is flammable and how it will react to fire.

Yeshua's Resurrection

Yeshua*: "The Son of man shall be betrayed into the hands of men: And they shall kill him, and the third day he shall be raised again. And they were exceeding sorry." **Matthew 17:22-23 KJV***

Shaul*: "For I delivered to you first of all that which I also received: that Christ died for our sins according to the Scriptures, and that He was buried, and that He rose again the third day according to the Scriptures" (**1 Corinthians 15:3-4 NKJV**).*

Judgment and Rewards

Yeshua*: "For the Son of Man is going to come in the glory of His Father with His angels; and will then recompense every man according to his deeds" (**Matthew 16:27 KJV**).*

Shaul: "God will give to each person according to what he has done" (**Romans 2:6 NIV**).

Sin of Man

Yeshua: "For out of the heart come evil thoughts—murder, adultery, sexual immorality, theft, false testimony, slander. 20 These are what defile a person; but eating with unwashed hands does not defile them" (**Matthew 15:19-20 NIV**).

Shaul: "There is no one who understands; there is no one who seeks God. All have turned away; they have together become worthless; there is no one who does good, not even one" (**Romans 3:11-12 NIV**).

Tradition Versus Obedience

Yeshua: "And why do you break the command of God for the sake of your tradition" (**Matthew 15:3 NIV**)?

Shaul: "See to it that no one takes you captive through philosophy and empty deception, according to the tradition of men, according to the elementary principles of the world, rather than according to Christ" (**Colossians 2:8 NASB**).

Faith Without Works

Yeshua: "On that day many will say to me, 'Lord, Lord, did we not prophesy in your name, and cast out demons in your name, and do many mighty works in your name?' And then will I declare to them, 'I never knew you; depart from me, you workers of lawlessness'" (**Matthew 7:22-23 ESV**).

Shaul: "Clearly no one is justified before God by the law, because, the righteous will live by faith" (**Galatians 3:11 NIV**).

THE FOUR TYPES OF LAWS

*C*olossians 2:13-14 has been used to justify the abandonment of the Torah or its observance by many in the Christian world today.

> *When you were dead in your sins and in the uncircumcision of your sinful nature, God made you alive with Christ. He forgave us all our sins, having canceled the written code, with its regulations, that was against us and that stood opposed to us; he took it away, nailing it to the cross (**Colossians 2:13-14 NIV**).*

These verses mention nothing about the law being nailed to the cross only the written code of ordinances. What then is the written code of ordinances? God gave **four types of laws to Israel** and all the Gentiles who stood at the mountain of God (Sinai). Understanding these four types of laws is the key to understanding this Scripture.

1. **The Ten Commandments**: The great universal moral law written by the very finger of God. The Ten Commandments are God's constitution for the government of and the entire universe. The Ten Commandments have been in effect ever since God was and will be in effect throughout all eternity, as long as God exists. These commandments touch the Holy

of Holies and the heart of God. To have any kind of understanding of God, one must understand the everlasting nature of His laws. These commandments show the very nature of His character and are integral to His righteousness. For Adonai to do away with these laws would be to do away with Himself.

2. **The Ceremonial Laws**: These laws pertain to the sacrifices and rituals that pertain to the service of the temple. These laws instruct the priests and community in the acceptable way to bring sacrifices to appease God's wrath. It is these laws Shaul refers to as the ordinances. They specifically pertain to sacrifices. Adonai planned from the beginning that the ceremonial laws would cease at the tree (cross) when Yeshua would become the ultimate sacrifice as the true Lamb of God. The animal sacrifices all pointed forward to Yeshua's death. Without the shedding of blood there could be no remission for sin. The animal sacrifices prior to Yeshua covered the people's sin and allowed a visible picture of His future sacrifice. Since Yeshua's death and the destruction of the temple in 70 AD, the laws that pertain to temple services are null and void. But those laws do not affect the moral law which is untouched.

3. **The Health or Hygiene Laws**: These are laws that govern health and hygiene which were given to guard, protect and guide us to holiness. The physics of the human body have not changed since creation or since these laws were given. The health laws are just as much a benefit for us today as they were for Israel. Consider the black plague of Europe when millions of Gentiles died because of the unsanitary way they lived. The plague did not affect the Jewish community as much as the general population because they followed God's regulations in the book of Leviticus regarding hygiene. Later in history the Gentile community rose up to kill the Jews, claiming that it was a Jewish plot that caused the black plague in Europe that killed hundreds of thousands.

Even today in many cultures and underdeveloped countries, disease is rampant where simple Biblical hygiene practices are not followed.

4.   **The Civil or Judicial Laws**: These laws govern the civil penalties for crimes within the theocracy of Israel. They also guide our approach and service to God. When someone is convicted of murder for instance, the murderer should be put to death swiftly to discourage others from this sin. The appointed judges made policies based on the commands of Moshe. The judicial laws regulating courts of justice are contained in the Torah. Dealings that pertain to the ceremonial law might be changed at the discretion of the judges' points of view based on the laws prescribed in the Torah. The judicial law of the Hebrews was adapted to protect the holiness and integrity of the Hebrew civil society.

The four types of laws listed above are the basis for the collective writings called the Torah. Each type of law has its place and purpose in human affairs. There is a difference between the law of God and the ordinances of God. Shaul upholds the legitimacy of the law.

Whosoever committeth sin transgresseth also the law: for sin is the transgression of the law (1 John 3:4 KJV).

*Do we then make void the law through faith? God forbid: yea, **we establish the law (Romans 3:31 KJV)**.*

A law that is established is not abolished or nailed to the cross. Has the law been established, or has it been nailed to the cross and abolished? Which is it? Obviously there is more than one type of law referred to here in Shaul's writings.

Man, as God's creation, was given the law. This shows man as something special, elevated and separate from the rest of creation. The law was given to men as a fence to differentiate men from the rest of God's creation. Yeshua sculpted man in His image from dirt. To be created in the image of God includes the knowledge of morality, choice and intellect that the animal kingdom does not have.

One of the problems with words such as *law, ordinances, covenants* and *precepts* in the New Testament is that it is often not clear which law or covenant is being referred to. But in each case God has given us a way to know which law or covenant is meant. Here we get into the challenge of understanding the Bible, which requires the use of the tools God gave Israel to understand the mysteries in the Word of God. The tools God gave Israel are:

- Hebrew language
- Hebraic (Biblical) customs
- Hebrew idioms
- Proper study of the Bible
- The command to Shmor (guard) the Shabbats

The prophet Isaiah gave these instructions on how to study the Bible:

> *For precept must be upon precept, precept upon precept; line upon line, line upon line; here a little, and there a little (Isaiah 28:10 KJV).*

If there is direct opposition then it is a lie. If one thing is true and another states the opposite, then one is true and one is not true. They both cannot be true. This is an antithesis. One is true; one is a lie.

> *God is not a man, that he should lie, nor a son of man, that he should change his mind. Does he speak and then not act? Does he promise and not fulfill? (Numbers 23:19 NIV)*

> *. . .a faith and knowledge resting on the hope of eternal life, which God, who does not lie, promised before the beginning of time. . . (Titus 1:2 NIV).*

> *God did this so that, by two unchangeable things in which it is impossible for God to lie, we who have fled to take hold of*

*the hope offered to us may be greatly encouraged (**Hebrews 6:18 NIV**).*

God cannot lie and God makes no mistakes. His laws were known before the world began and they were perfect. Since it is impossible for God to lie and contradictions are lies, there can be no contradictions anywhere in the Bible.

> ***All Scripture is God-breathed*** *[or spoken] and is useful **for teaching, rebuking, correcting** and **training** in righteousness, so that the man of God may be **thoroughly equipped for every good work** (2 **Timothy 3:16-17 NIV**).*

When these verses were penned, the New Testament had not been written. This statement (yet to be canonized) is referring to the Old Testament as the texts profitable for doctrine, reproof, correction and instruction in righteousness.

> *The works of his hands are verity and judgment; **all his commandments are sure**. They stand fast forever and ever, and are done in truth and uprightness. He sent redemption unto his people: **he hath commanded his covenant forever**: holy and reverend is his name (**Psalm 111:7-9 NIV**).*

We are told very plainly that all of God's Ten Commandments will stand fast, forever and ever. This is very important when people think the New Testament speaks of a covenant or a law that was discontinued. It cannot possibly refer to the Torah or covenants relating to the **Ten Commandments.**

> *Remember the Sabbath day by keeping it holy. Six days you shall labor and do all your work, but the seventh day is a Sabbath to the LORD your God. On it you shall not do any work, neither you, nor your son or daughter, nor your manservant or maidservant, nor your animals, nor the alien within your gates. For in six days the LORD made the heavens and the earth, the sea, and all that is in them, but he*

*rested on the seventh day. Therefore the LORD blessed the Sabbath day and made it holy (**Exodus 20:8-11 NIV**).*

One of the Ten Commandments covers the Shabbat. At the end of the six days of creation, God blessed and **sanctified the seventh day**. God never blessed, sanctified, or made holy any other day of the week. **Ecclesiastes 3:14** is clear that God's seventh day (Saturday), will remain blessed, sanctified and holy throughout all eternity. Why is the Sabbath so critical to understand? God existed before creation and we know from Scripture that God is eternal. He is also the Shabbat, or we can call the Shabbat by another name—eternity.

*I know that everything God does will endure forever; nothing can be added to it and nothing taken from it. God does it so that men will revere him (**Ecclesiastes 3:14 NIV**).*

King Shlomo (Solomon) makes it clear that Adonai will never change or abolish his Ten Commandments or his Shabbat day. Many people twist these clear Bible texts by saying that these verses are figurative language, or the verses are spiritual, or that forever does not really mean forever, or that they are only for the Jews.

Using Shaul's writings to justify their positions, many Christians today claim that the Ten Commandments were only for the Jews, but they are quick to admit that lying, stealing and adultery are all sins. The Shabbat is the one commandment not followed. These are the only commandments in the Bible that God Himself wrote with His finger on Mount Sinai with Moshe. He wrote them to show us their importance and to make us realize that they are eternal. Most of the laws given to Moshe were written on parchment from a living Kosher animal which points to their temporary use, while the Ten Commandments were written in stone by the very finger of Adonai showing their permanence.

The laws of God were hidden from men in a golden box called The Ark of the Covenant guarded by the heavenly bodies, the cherubim—the very angels that guarded the entrance to the Garden of Eden to protect and preserve it for a future use. The cherubim also guarded the body of Yeshua until the resurrection before He was revealed to the world.

> . . .*and saw two angels in white, seated where Jesus's body had been, one at the head and the other at the foot (**John 20:12**).*

God wrote the Ten Commandments on stone to show their permanence, just as Yeshua is called the Rock of all Ages. He is the Word, the embodiment of the Ten Commandments. He gave it, He lived by it, He taught it and it is He. Yeshua Himself tells us to live by every word that comes out of the mouth of God.

> *But he answered and said, "**It is written**, Man shall not live by bread alone, **but by every word that proceeds out of the mouth of God**" (**Matthew 4:4 NASB**).*

Moshe received the law directly face to face from the mouth of God while the finger of God inscribed the Ten Commandments. The Ten Commandments are an abbreviation of the law and foundation on which all of the Torah stands. It is not only about killing and stealing, it is about proper human interaction. To love our neighbor is just one law but it has many branches. To love God is one law but it has many branches as well. It is left for us to study and search the Scriptures to find eternal life.

> *You search the Scriptures because you think **that in them you have eternal life;** it is the Scriptures that testify about Me; and you are unwilling to come to Me so that you may have life (**John 5:39-40 KJV**).*

Which is more weighty or important in the Bible, the words that came from God Himself, or the words of Shaul, a mere creation of God?

DECREES AND ORDINANCES

*T*here are thousands of known religions in the world. All of them (save one, Judaism), base their claim on the personal revelation of an individual's dream or vision. A personal revelation is when one person claims to have received a special message from an angel or his or her god, writes it down and then proceeds to share this revelation with others resulting in a massive following. With a personal revelation, there is no way to verify what really happened; you just have to take the person at their word.

Why would God establish His relationship with people He created without the possibility of verification? How could God then expect these people to obediently follow a code of instructions, based solely on the word of one person? Judaism is the only religion in recorded history that makes the claim that a whole nation heard God speak. No other religion claims the experience of national revelation. God then claims in Deuteronomy that there will never be another national claim like this.

> *You might inquire about times long past, from the day that God created man on earth, and from one end of heaven to the other: Has there ever been anything like this great thing or has anything like it been heard? Have a people ever heard the voice of God speaking from the midst of the fires as you have heard and survived? (**Deut. 4:32-33**)*

The Torah claims that the entire nation heard God speak at Mount Sinai. God did not just appear to Moses individually in a private hut; He appeared to everyone—a nation of about three million people witnessed God speaking first hand. This claim is mentioned many times in the Torah and other documents of the neighboring nations.

Moses warned the Israelites to remember:

Only beware for yourself and greatly beware for your soul, ***lest you forget the things that your eyes have beheld. Do not remove this memory from your heart all the days of your life. Teach your children and your children's children about the day that you stood before the Lord your God at Horev [Mount Sinai] (Genesis 4:9).***

God spoke to you from the midst of the fire, you were hearing the sound of words, but you were not seeing a form, only a sound. He told you of His covenant, instructing you to keep the Ten Commandments, and He inscribed them on two stone tablets ***(Deut. 4:10-13).***

You have been shown in order to know that God, He is the Supreme Being. There is none besides Him. From heaven he let you hear His voice in order to teach you, and on earth He showed you His great fire, and you heard His words amid the fire ***(Deut. 4:32-36).***

Moses called all of Israel and said to them: "Hear, O Israel, the decrees and the ordinances that I speak in your ears today—learn them, and be careful to perform them. The Lord your God sealed a covenant with us at Horev [Mount Sinai]. ***Not with our forefathers did God seal this covenant, but with us****—we who are here, all of us alive today.* ***Face to face did God speak with you*** *on the mountain from amid the fire"* ***(Deut. 5:1-4).***

The Torah claims that the entire Jewish nation heard God speak at Sinai, a claim that has been accepted as part of their nation's history for over three thousand years. This is the origin of the Ten Commandments.

THE TEN COMMANDMENTS

*T*he Ten Commandments of God are His constitution for the universe, which are enshrined in His temple in heaven. The ark in heaven is the same ark that the Ark of the Covenant was patterned after which contains the Ten Commandments.

> *And the temple of God was opened in heaven, and there was seen in his temple the ark of his testament (**Revelation 11:19 KJV**).*

> *Who serve unto the example and shadow of heavenly things, as Moses was admonished of God when he was about to make the tabernacle: for, See, saith he, that thou make all things according to the pattern showed to thee in the mount (**Hebrews 8:5 KJV**).*

The Ten Commandments existed before Mt. Sinai, before Avraham, before creation itself. We know that Satan sinned in heaven before creation began. To have sinned in heaven entails laws or commandments of God that were in force and broken by Satan while the earth was still formless and void. If there were no laws in heaven, how could God, who is just and righteous, throw Satan out for disobedience to the law? When Adam and Ha'yah (Eve) sinned in the Garden of Eden it was in direct disobedience to a stated law. It was disobedience to God's law that caused man to lose paradise on earth.

The Ten Commandments are a written form of the character of God. He holds the world together and creation could not exist without his character expressed in the Ten Commandments. They were established before man was created and will be the measure of our judgment. Avraham lived by the laws of God over four hundred years before the giving of the Torah on the Mount. He was found righteous in Adonai's eyes according to the laws of God.

> . . .*because Abraham obeyed me and did everything I required of him, keeping my commands, my decrees and my instructions"* (**Genesis 26:5 NIV**).

> *If he did not spare the ancient world when he brought the flood on its ungodly people, but protected Noah, a preacher of righteousness, and seven others"* (**2 Peter 2:5 NIV**).

Noah preached to the world for five hundred years before the flood about God's righteousness, plus one hundred years during the building of the ark. Noah learned about God's righteousness from the oral lessons handed down from Adam. Yeshua visited Adam on a daily basis and the visitation no doubt consisted of Yeshua teaching Adam the righteousness of God. The Ten Commandments were part of the Torah lesson and after the fall, Adam shared his experience with his children, grandchildren and great-grandchildren. The lessons taught to Adam were passed down to all the generations prior to the flood all the way to Moses, who wrote the Pentateuch.

Ten generations separate Adam from Noah. Ten is the number of righteousness, but instead of civilizations learning from the mistakes of Adam, humanity progressively became vile and corrupt turning away from God. As a result, God destroyed the world with a flood, preserving only Noah, his family and enough animals to replenish the earth once again.

Noah found grace in the eyes of the Lord. He was a just man and walked in righteousness with God. Noah's walk of righteousness was long before the Jewish people existed as a covenant group, long before the giving of the Torah to Moshe on Mount Sinai. Noah walked in obedience to God's commands and preached righteousness for one hundred years. Today, just as in the days of Noah, people mock the teachers of the Torah, right up until it is too late to repent. Is there a lesson in all of this for us today?

The Scriptures are clear that the Ten Commandments began before creation and will remain in effect forever as they portray the very nature of God. Even until the very end of the age, Satan and his minions attack those who keep God's commandments as written in Revelation.

> *And the dragon was wroth with the woman, and went to make war with the remnant of her seed, which keep the commandments of God, and have the testimony of Yeshua (**Revelation 12:17 KJV**).*

> *Here is the patience of the Saints: here are they that keep the commandments of God, and the faith of Yeshua (**Revelation 14:12: KJV**).*

> *Blessed are they that do His commandments (**Revelation 22:14 KJV**).*

The Word of God does not have a portion that is new, nor is a section old and outdated. To address His Word as the Old Testament or the New Testament is to distinguish between time periods, not to say that one is outdated and one has new revelation. The Old Testament is not outdated and nothing is new in the New Testament. The New Testament is a fulfillment of the previous promises made to the fathers and prophets of Israel. There was a Savior born in Israel, as was foretold. The prophets predicted the place, the time and the condition of His birth. When the right time came and the Savior Yeshua was born, it was recorded by the scribes of that day, which included the twelve disciples chosen to record His deeds and continue with the mission He started.

Just as Yeshua entrusted Moshe and the twelve sons of Israel with His Torah at Sinai, so did this same Yeshua entrust His twelve disciples to take the message to the ends of the world. The Ten Commandments are reiterated in the New Testament. Consider comparison of these verses from the Old Testament with the New Testament.

1. *"You shall have no other gods before me" (**Exodus 20:3 NIV**).*
   - *"Yeshua said to him, "Away from me, Satan! For it is written: 'Worship the Lord your God, and serve him only'" (**Matthew 4:10 NIV**).*
   - *"No one can serve two masters. Either he will hate the one and love the other, or he will be devoted to the one and despise the other. You cannot serve both God and Money" (**Matthew 6:24 NIV**).*

2. *"You shall not make for yourself an idol in the form of anything in heaven above or on the earth beneath or in the waters below. You shall not bow down to them or worship them; for I, the LORD your God, am a jealous God, punishing the children for the sin of the fathers to the third and fourth generation of those who hate me, but showing love to a thousand generations of those who love me and keep my commandments"(**Exodus 20:4-6 NIV**).*
   - *"Instead we should write to them, telling them to abstain from food polluted by idols, from sexual immorality, from the meat of strangled animals and from blood" (**Acts 15:20 NIV**).*
   - *"Do not be idolaters, as some of them were; as it is written: "The people sat down to eat and drink and got up to indulge in pagan revelry" (**1 Corinthians 10:7 NIV**).*

3. *"You shall not misuse the name of the LORD your God, for the LORD will not hold anyone guiltless who misuses his name" (**Exodus 20:7 NIV**).*
   - *"This, then, is how you should pray: "'Our Father in heaven, hallowed be your name," (**Matthew 6:9 NIV**)*

- *"All who are under the yoke of slavery should consider their masters worthy of full respect, so that God's name and our teaching may not be slandered"* (**1 Timothy 6:1 NIV**).

4. *"Remember the Sabbath day by keeping it holy. Six days you shall labor and do all your work, but the seventh day is a Sabbath to the LORD your God. On it you shall not do any work, neither you, nor your son or daughter, nor your manservant or maidservant, nor your animals, nor the alien within your gates. For in six days the LORD made the heavens and the earth, the sea, and all that is in them, but he rested on the seventh day. Therefore the LORD blessed the Sabbath day and made it holy"* (**Exodus 20:8-11 NIV**).
   - *"For the Son of Man is Lord of the Sabbath"* (**Matthew 12:8 NIV**).
   - *"There remains, then, a Sabbath-rest for the people of God; for anyone who enters God's rest also rests from his own work, just as God did from his. Let us, therefore, make every effort to enter that rest, so that no one will fall by following their example of disobedience"* (**Hebrews 4:9-11 NIV**).

5. *"Honor your father and your mother, so that you may live long in the land the LORD your God is giving you"* (**Exodus 20:12 NIV**).
   - *"For Moses said, 'Honor your father and your mother,' and, 'Anyone who curses his father or mother must be put to death"* (**Mark 7:10 NIV**).
   - *"Children, obey your parents in everything, for this pleases the Lord"* (**Colossians 3:20 NIV**).

6. *"You shall not murder"* (**Exodus 20:13 NIV**).
   - *""You have heard that it was said to the people long ago, 'Do not murder, and anyone who murders will be subject to judgment.'* [22] *But I tell you that anyone who is angry with his brother will be subject to judgment.*

Again, anyone who says to his brother, 'Raca, [empty or air head] 'is answerable to the Sanhedrin. But anyone who says, 'You fool!' will be in danger of the fire of hell" (**Matthew 5:21-22 NIV**).

- *The commandments, "Do not commit adultery, do not murder, do not steal, do not covet," and whatever other commandment there may be, are summed up in this one rule: "Love your neighbor as yourself"* (**Romans 13:9 NIV**).

7. *"You shall not commit adultery"* (**Exodus 20:14 NIV**).
    - *"Which ones?" the man inquired. Jesus replied, "'Do not murder, do not commit adultery, do not steal, do not give false testimony,"* (**Matthew 19:18 NIV**)
    - *"So then, if she marries another man while her husband is still alive, she is called an adulteress. But if her husband dies, she is released from that law and is not an adulteress, even though she marries another man"* (**Romans 7:3 NIV**).

8. *"You shall not steal"* (**Exodus 20:15 NIV**).
    - *"You know the commandments: 'Do not commit adultery, do not murder, do not steal, do not give false testimony,' honor your father and mother'"* (**Luke 18:20 NIV**).
    - *". . .nor thieves nor the greedy nor drunkards nor slanderers nor swindlers will inherit the kingdom of God"* (**1 Corinthians 6:10 NIV**).

9. *"You shall not give false testimony against your neighbor"* (**Exodus 20:16 NIV**).
    - *"For out of the heart come evil thoughts, murder, adultery, sexual immorality, theft, false testimony, slander"* (**Matthew 15:19 NIV**).
    - *"Therefore each of you must put off falsehood and speak truthfully to his neighbor, for we are all members of one body"* (**Ephesians 4:25 NIV**).

10. *"You shall not covet your neighbor's house. You shall not covet your neighbor's wife, or his manservant or maidservant, his ox or donkey, or anything that belongs to your neighbor" (**Exodus 20:17 NIV**).*
    - *"Then he said to them, 'Watch out! Be on your guard against all kinds of greed; a man's life does not consist in the abundance of his possessions'" (**Luke 12:15 NIV**).*
    - *"For the love of money is a root of all kinds of evil. Some people, eager for money, have wandered from the faith and pierced themselves with many grief's" (**1 Timothy 6:10 NIV**).*

The Ten Commandments define righteousness and all the commandments are righteous. Righteousness is keeping the commandments.

*My tongue shall speak of your word: for all your commandments are righteousness (**Psalm 119:172 KJV**).*

*And it shall be our righteousness, if we observe to do all these commandments before the Lord our God, as he has commanded us (**Deuteronomy 6:25 KJV**).*

Raise your eyes toward the skies, look at the earth below. The skies will vanish like smoke, the earth will wear out like clothing. Those living on it will die like flies; but my salvation will be forever, and my justice will never end. "Listen to me, you who know justice, you people who have my Torah in your heart: don't."

*"Hear me, you who know what is right, you people who have taken my instruction to heart: Do not fear the reproach of mere mortals or be terrified by their insults" (**Isaiah 51:6-7**).*

The Ten Commandments are the righteousness of God and they shall never be abolished.

YESHUA AND THE LAW

The origin of Yeshua helps us understand the origin of the law.

*In the beginning was the Word and the Word was with God and the Word was God (**John 1:1 NIV**).*

*I*f the word became flesh and dwelt among us, then the Word speaks of Yeshua's life on earth. He is the Word, which is the righteousness of God His Father. Yeshua is the Word, the Spirit of God and the law. If Shaul somehow was teaching his generation about doing away with the law, he then was also teaching us to do away with Yeshua. If that is the case, living out from under the law of God is living without Yeshua as well. To live out from under the law, which John says is Yeshua, ultimately separates us from God's salvation power and destines us to eternal death.

*Think not that I am come to destroy the law, or the prophets: **I am not come to destroy, but to fulfill**. For verily I say unto you, till heaven and earth pass, one jot or one tittle shall in no wise pass from the law, till all be fulfilled (**Matthew 5:17-18 KJV**).*

The gravity and power of **Matthew 5:17-18** is Yeshua declaring that He did not come to destroy but fulfill the Torah and that the law will not pass away as long as there is a heaven and earth, day and night. The Jews were very precise with every letter and stroke when writing a new Torah scroll. The smallest mistake, change, or omission would mean they had to destroy the entire column or portion and start over. Not only is Yeshua saying that the smallest part of the law will never be changed or omitted—Yeshua is saying that all of the Torah law will be fulfilled. There is no other law that Yeshua is talking about except those laws given by God to Israel at Mt. Sinai—more specifically, the Ten Commandments.

If Yeshua does away with the law, then He is doing away with Himself. He is the Word (the law giver) that became flesh. He came to establish Himself. He came to fulfill that which was prophesied from Genesis to Malachi. He walked the earth to feel pain, sorrow, emotions and ultimately die. He came to fulfill all areas of everyday life and overcome them in order to deliver us from sin and make us victorious.

> *But now in Mashiach Yeshua you who once were far away have been brought near through the blood of Mashiach [**life is in the blood**]. For he himself is our peace, who has made the two one and has destroyed the barrier, the dividing wall of hostility, by abolishing in his flesh the law [**Torah**] with its commandments and regulations [**sacrifices**]. His purpose was to create in himself one new man out of the two, thus making peace [**one walk, one faith, one God**]. . . (Ephesians 2:13-15 NIV).*

Yeshua fulfilled the law by demonstrating perfect obedience to every one of the commandments given to Moses on top of the mountain. It was His perfect obedience that made Him the perfect sacrifice. **He did not abolish the law; He fulfilled the Law of Ordinances, the Law of Sacrifice.** The verses we just read show this clearly. There is only one law given and only one Savior for mankind and His name is Yeshua. The Lord of the Old Testament is the Mashiah of the New Testament.

*You are my witnesses, says the Lord, and my servant whom I have chosen: that you may know and believe me, and understand that I am he: before me there was no God formed, neither shall there be after me. I, even I, am the Lord; and beside me there is no savior (**Isaiah 43:10-11 KJV**).*

*There is one lawgiver, who is able to save and to destroy: who are you that judges another? (**James 4:12 KJ**)*

Since Yeshua is the only lawgiver, the commandments and the law of Yeshua are one and the same.

*Carry each other's burdens, and in this way you will fulfill the law of Christ (**Galatians 6:2 NIV**).*

Not only is Yeshua the only lawgiver, He is also the Creator.

*In the beginning was the Word, and the Word was with God, and the Word was God. **He was with God in the beginning. Through him all things were made**; without him nothing was made that has been made (**John 1:1-3 NIV**).*

*He is the image of the invisible God, the firstborn over all creation. **For by him all things were created: things in heaven and on earth**, visible and invisible, whether thrones or powers or rulers or authorities; all things were created by him and for him. He is before all things, and in him all things hold together (**Colossians 1:15-17 NIV**).*

To intentionally break the commandments of God is to crucify Yeshua and nullify His sacrifice. It is to deny the One who is acting on the behalf of the Almighty; the One who created everything; the One that gave the Torah—the One who died to reunite man with His Father.

*Whoever commits sin transgresses also the law: for **sin is the transgression of the law** (1 John 3:4 AKJ).*

*And have tasted the good word of God, and the powers of the world to come, If they shall fall away, to renew them again unto repentance; seeing they crucify to themselves the Son of God afresh, and put him to an open shame (**Hebrews 6:5-6 KJV**).*

*For if we sin willfully after that we have received the knowledge of the truth, there remaineth no more sacrifice for sin (**Hebrews 10:26 KJV**).*

If the law was done away with, what constitutes sin? If there are no boundaries, how do we know we have broken them? In order to determined sin there must be a law that dictates what is acceptable to God and what is rejected by God. Sin is breaking God's commandments. People who say the law is passed away regardless of the reason are throwing away the very boundary that protects us from sin. What is sin without the law of God to make the distinction?

Yeshua's words in **Matthew 5:17-18** do not exist in a vacuum by themselves. There is a consistent and clear pattern in the Torah of God that demonstrates the law is in full force and requires obedience.

*Do not think that I have come to abolish the Law or the Prophets; I have not come to abolish them but to fulfill them. For truly I tell you, until heaven and earth disappear, not the smallest letter, not the least stroke of a pen, will by any means disappear from the Law until everything is accomplished (**Matthew 5:17-18 NIV**).*

*Anyone who breaks one of the least of these commandments and teaches others to do the same will be called least in the kingdom of heaven, but whoever practices and teaches these commands will be called great in the kingdom of heaven (**Matthew 5:19 NIV**).*

*It is easier for heaven and earth to disappear than for the least stroke of a pen to drop out of the Law (**Luke 16:17 NIV**).*

*Now a man [lawyer] came up to Yeshua and asked, "Teacher, [rabbi] what good thing must I do to get eternal life?" "Why do you ask me about what is good?" Yeshua replied. "There is only One who is good. If you want to enter life, obey the commandments." "Which ones?" the man inquired. Yeshua replied, "Do not murder, do not commit adultery, do not steal, do not give false testimony, honor your father and mother," and 'love your neighbor as yourself'" (**Matthew 19:16-19 NIV**).*

Yeshua confirms the Torah when teaching in Matthew that the two overriding love concepts originate from the Ten Commandments that govern all the Torah.

*Thou shalt love the Lord thy God with all thy heart, and with all thy soul, and with all thy mind. This is the first and great commandment. And the second is like unto it, Thou shalt love thy neighbor as thyself. On these two commandments hang all the law and the prophets (**Matthew 22:37-40 KJV**).*

It was foretold that Yeshua would bring the law to the Gentiles.

*Here is my servant, whom I uphold, my chosen one in whom I delight; I will put my spirit on him and he will bring justice [Torah] to the nations (**Isaiah 42:1 NIV**).*

Justice can only be obtained if there is law in place. If there is no law, there is nothing to judge and if there is nothing to judge, there is no need for justice or for a savior. All the courts of the world are guided by a set of laws in order to judge and hand down a sentence or a verdict of justice.

*For the priest's lips should keep knowledge, and they should **seek the law at his mouth:** for he is the messenger of the LORD of hosts. But **ye are departed out of the way; ye have caused many to stumble at the law;** ye have corrupted* *the covenant of Levi, saith the LORD of hosts (**Malachi 2:7-8 NIV**).*

*Nevertheless I tell you the truth; It is expedient for you that I go away: for if I go not away, the Comforter will not come unto you; but if I depart, I will send him unto you. And **when he is come, he will reprove the world of sin, and of righteousness, and of judgment:** (**John 16:7-8 NIV**)*

*Not everyone who says to me, "Lord, Lord," will enter the kingdom of heaven, but only the one who does the will of my Father who is in heaven. Many will say to me on that day, 'Lord, Lord, did we not prophesy in your name and in your name drive out demons and in your name perform many miracles?' Then I will tell them plainly, "I never knew you. Away from me, you evildoers! **Therefore everyone who hears these words of mine and puts them into practice is like a wise man who built his house on the rock.** The rain came down, the streams rose, and the winds blew and beat against that house; yet it did not fall, because it had its foundation on the rock. But everyone who hears these words of mine and does not put them into practice is like a foolish man who built his house on sand. The rain came down, the streams rose, and the winds blew and beat against that house, and it fell with a great crash." When Jesus had finished saying these things, the crowds were amazed at his teaching, because he taught as one who had authority, and not as their teachers of the law (**Matthew 7:21-29 NIV**).*

*My dear children, I write this to you so that you will not sin. But if anybody does sin, we have an advocate with the Father—Jesus Christ, the **[Tzaddik]** Righteous One. He is the atoning sacrifice for our sins, and not only for ours but also for the sins of the whole world. **We know that we have come to know him if we keep his commands. Whoever says, "I know him," but does not do what he commands is a liar, and the truth is not in that person.** But if anyone obeys his* *word, love for God is truly made complete in them. This is how we know we are in him: Whoever claims to live in him must live as Jesus did.* **Dear friends, I am not writing you a new command but an old one, which you have had since the beginning. This old command is the message you have heard** *(1 John 2:1-7 NIV).*

Everyone who keeps sinning is violating Torah, indeed, *sin is violation of Torah. You know that he appeared in order to take away sins, and that there is no sin in him. So* **no one who remains united with him continues sinning; everyone who does continue sinning has neither seen him nor known him.** *Children, don't let anyone deceive you;* **it is the person that keeps on doing what is right who is righteous, just as God is righteous. The person who keeps on sinning is from the adversary, because from the very beginning the adversary has kept on sinning [seared conscience].** *It was for this very reason that the Son of God appeared, to destroy these doings of the Adversary* **(1 John 3:4-8 NIV).**

. . .and receive from him anything we ask, because we keep his commands and do what pleases him. And this is his command: to believe in the name of his Son, Jesus Christ, and to love one another as he commanded us. The one who keeps God's commands lives in him, and he in them. And this is how we know that he lives in us: We know it by the Spirit he gave us **(1 John 3:22-24 NIV).**

It is the law that directed us to Yeshua and it is Yeshua who gave it to us in the desert of Sinai through Moshe. The Torah is and has been our teacher, showing us the will of the Father through Yeshua. The Torah introduced us to the Word that became flesh and dwelt among us. Without the law we would never have understood the will of God the Father. Only through the law do we understand the role and the purpose of the Messiah.

Do we reject the law, the Torah, just because Yeshua came? God forbid. We cling to the law for it is our fence, our boundary and defense. It teaches us how to approach the Master. It teaches us godly etiquette. It is the Torah, the laws of God that allow us to know Yeshua. If we reject the Torah, we reject Yeshua who is our only salvation.

> *We know that we have come to know him if we obey his commands.* **The man who says, "I know him," but does not do what he commands is a liar,** *and the truth is not in him. But if anyone obeys his word, God's love is truly made complete in him. This is how we know we are in him: Whoever claims to live in him must walk as Yeshua did* **(1 John 2:3-6 NIV).**

It is by keeping the laws of God we become like Yeshua. That is how He will know His people upon His return. He will see us keeping His laws as He did.

John 17 is known as the Lord's Prayer. In this prayer, Yeshua is using a powerful and unusual request. In the synagogues Jews recite this prayer, "Shma Israel Adonai Eloheynu, Adonai **Echad.**" Yeshua begs that His followers be **Echad**, meaning, *"Make them one even as we are one."*

> *I have given them the glory that you gave me, that they may be one as we are one* **(John 17:22 NIV).**

> *However, if you suffer as a Christian, do not be ashamed, but praise God that you bear that name. For it is time for judgment to begin with God's household; and if it begins with us, what will the outcome be for those who do not obey the gospel of God? And, "If it is hard for the righteous to be saved, what will become of the ungodly and the sinner?"* **(1 Peter 4:16-18 NIV)**

Consider the weight of the words in the verses above, warning that judgment starts with God's people. Without the law, we would be like the sons of Aaron who were burned because they brought their own/strange fire to the altar. They brought what they thought would be pleasing to God. It was not done with bad intention, just the opposite, but it was not done according to the Torah or by the will of God.

We are commissioned to find out the will of God, but unfortunately we do not have the person of Yeshua here with us today. So the closest thing to Yeshua we have today is His word, the Torah. Only the Torah can show us the perfect will of God. All the prophecies of the Bible and their fulfillment are based on the laws of God. How can a person claim they believe in prophecy, yet they do not believe in God's laws? Prophecy is based on God's laws. To deny the law of God is to also deny prophecy.

The law that was given to Israel in the days of the wilderness is the same law that was kept in Yerushalaim (Jerusalem). These same laws will be observed under Yeshua when He returns and restores His future temple in Yerushalaim (Jerusalem):

> *The law and the Prophets were proclaimed until John. Since that time, the good news of the kingdom of God is being preached, and everyone is forcing his way into it* (**Luke 16:16 NIV**).

Some people interpret this Scripture to suggest the law only exists up till Yochanan (John). Yet, rudimentary study of any part of the New Testament shows otherwise.

The real meaning of **Luke 16:16** is that no other prophets could add or abolish God's laws. The law was given until Yochanan and no one could change it. It doesn't mean that we are to live in an ungodly, chaotic state of lawlessness. If Yeshua's statement meant to dispel God's laws from humanity, then it would directly contradict His statements about the permanence of the law and the effect of His presence on the law.

> *It is easier for heaven and earth to disappear than for the least stroke of a pen to drop out of the law* (**Luke 16:17 NIV**).
>
> **Do not think that I have come to abolish the law or the prophets; I have not come to abolish them but to fulfill them.** *I tell you the truth, until heaven and earth disappear,*

*not the smallest letter, not the least stroke of a pen, will by any means disappear from the Law until everything is accomplished. Anyone who breaks one of the least of these commandments and teaches others to do the same will be called least in the kingdom of heaven, but whoever practices and teaches these commands will be called great in the kingdom of heaven (**Matthew 5:17-19 NIV**).*

Yeshua warned us about false prophets. He said that no one could change God's law. If it were true that Shaul taught another way to heaven, then he is a false prophet and his teachings should be rejected.

Did Yeshua die in order to set us free from the dreadful laws given to us by a loving God? Do we just believe that Yeshua is the Son of God and we will be saved, with no further walk of obedience? If there is no need to follow the laws that Yeshua gave us by the hand of Moshe and all we need to do is believe that Yeshua is the Son of God, then there is no need for us to go to the church or synagogue. We would not need anyone to teach us the Word of God since we are no longer "under any law." There is nothing we can say or do that will bring any consequence to sin.

If that were the case, will we just wait for Yeshua to come and take us to heaven while the people live as in the days of Noah? If there was a chance that people today could live in sin as in the days of Noah and still be saved, then we are not serving a righteous and Holy God. How could He justify drowning the entire generation of Noah (possibly three billion people) and spare us as we live in **sin**?

Finally, consider Yeshua's words about those who teach others to break even the least of the commandments:

> *Anyone who breaks one of the least of these commandments and teaches others to do the same will be called least in the kingdom of heaven, but whoever practices and teaches these commands will be called great in the kingdom of heaven (**Matthew 5:19 NIV**).*

117

God holds His rule over everything in this universe. He is sovereign over heaven and earth, life and death, good and evil. When Yeshua speaks of being the least in the kingdom of heaven when teaching others to break the Torah, it is not a good thing. Yet those who teach others to keep the Torah will be elevated to the highest in the kingdom of heaven. How can anyone think Yeshua or Shaul ever meant for people to do away with the laws of God?

> *And no wonder, for **Satan himself masquerades as an angel of light**. It is not surprising, then, if **his servants masquerade as servants of righteousness**. Their end will be what their actions deserve (**2 Corinthians 11:14-15 NIV**).*

> *Be self-controlled and alert. Your enemy the devil prowls around like a roaring lion looking for someone to devour (**1 Peter 5:8 NIV**).*

> *The great dragon was hurled down—that ancient serpent called the devil, or Satan, **who leads the whole world astray**. He was hurled to the earth, and his angels with him (**Revelation 12:9**).*

Circumcision of the Flesh and of the Heart

God's intent from the beginning was to have (Am Sgulah) a peculiar people who would be circumcised in the flesh and circumcised in the heart. The circumcision of the heart is the most important because it houses the very heart of man, our very soul and spirit. A holy heart needs to live in a holy house or body.

> *Any uncircumcised male who will not let himself be **circumcised** in the flesh of his foreskin—that person will be **cut off from his people**, because **he has broken my covenant** (**Genesis 17:14 NIV**).*

> *Circumcise your hearts, therefore, and do not be stiff-necked any longer" (**Deuteronomy 10:16 NIV**).*

118

*And a highway will be there; it will be called the Way of Holiness; it will be for those who walk on that Way. The unclean will not journey on it; wicked fools will not go about on it (**Isaiah 35:8 NIV**).*

*This is what the Sovereign LORD says: No foreigner **uncircumcised** in heart and flesh is to enter my sanctuary, not even the foreigners who live among the Israelites (**Ezekiel 44:9 NIV**).*

*And there shall in no wise enter into it anything **unclean**, or he that maketh an abomination and a lie: but only they that are written in the Lamb's book of life (**Revelation 21:27 ASV**).*

Being cut off from his people implies a divorce or an eternal separation from God's covenant. It would be the same as if he was stoned or hung. Each time the verse speaks of uncleanliness, it implies **man** and it always alludes to circumcision. If it were for a woman it would state NIDAH-separation or unclean by issue of her blood. There is no mistake; in the Hebrew it describes **man,** not woman.

UNDER THE LAW

When the New Testament refers to righteousness, you should automatically think of the commandments. The definition for righteousness rests with God's commandments. Some texts in the New Testament refer being under grace, not law. They speak of being justified. What does it mean to be under grace? What is the definition of grace?

> *And he said unto me, My grace is sufficient for thee: for my strength is made perfect in weakness. Most gladly therefore will I rather glory in my infirmities, that the power of Christ may rest upon me (**2 Corinthians 12:9 KJV**).*

Grace generally means favor, merciful or generous. There are many Old Testament references to finding favor with God and man. Grace is not an intangible concept; it is the act of seeking favor in God's eyes according to what God considers righteous. The Torah defines righteous acts that bring the favor of Adonai.

Every time the word justified is used in the Old Testament, it is translated from the Hebrew word *tzadaq*, which means, "made right or righteous." Every time the word *justified* is used in the New Testament it is translated from the Greek word *dikaioo*, which means "shown to be righteous." When we are justified, we are righteous. If a person is justified he is keeping the commandments of God:

> *That being justified by his grace [or goodness] we should*
> *be made heirs according to the hope of eternal life*
> *(**Titus 3:7 KJV**).*

Here we see that it is grace, or the mercy of Adonai, that gives us the power to obey the Torah. Without the favor or goodness of Adonai, the law will demand our death. So the goodness of Adonai is through His Son. He loved us so, He gave us His only Son to give us a second chance at repentance. By ourselves, without God's grace and power to keep us from sinning, it is impossible for us to obey the law. Shaul sums up the human condition in Romans:

> *For I know that in me (that is, in my flesh) dwells nothing*
> *good: for to will is present [now] with me; but how to per-*
> *form that which is good I find not. For the good that I would*
> *[should] I do not: but the evil, which I would [should] not,*
> *that I do (**Romans 7:18-19 KJV**).*

Concerning the New Covenant

> *"The time is coming," declares the LORD, "when I will*
> *make a new covenant with the house of Israel and with the*
> *house of Judah. It will not be like the covenant I made with*
> *their forefathers when I took them by the hand to lead them*
> *out of Egypt, because they broke my covenant, though I was*
> *a husband to them," declares the LORD. **"This is the cov-***
> ***enant I will make with the house of Israel after that time,"***
> ***declares the LORD. "I will put my law in their minds and***
> ***write it on their hearts. I will be their God, and they will be***
> ***my people"** (Jeremiah 31:31-33 NIV).*

This is a mighty promise God makes to His people. He says that He Himself will cause them to walk in His statutes. He will be the power, the love and grace in the lives of His people to cause them always to obey His commandments. Furthermore, He says that **all** His people will indeed keep His statutes and His laws.

Despite the overwhelming evidence for keeping the commandments of God, there is a verse used over and over to justify not keeping the commandments of Adonai.

> *For sin shall not be master over you, for you are not under law, but under grace. What then? Shall we sin because we are not under law but under grace? May it never be! Do you not know that when you present yourselves to someone as slaves for obedience, you are slaves of the one whom you obey, either of sin resulting in death, or of obedience resulting in righteousness?* **(Romans 6:14-16 NASB)**

What does it mean not to be under the law? Is Shaul really saying the law was abolished? Is Shaul really defying the very Son of God who said, *"If you love me, keep my commandments?"*

If it were true the Torah was done away with, are we free to lie, steal and cheat? In **Romans 6:15**, Shaul tells us it is possible to sin while not being under the law. *"What then? Shall we sin, because we are not under the law, but under grace? God forbid."* **1 John 3:4** specifies, *"Sin is the transgression of the law."* These verses tell us we can sin while we are not under the law. Therefore the law has certainly not been abolished.

It is like the son who is told to do something and chooses not to do it thinking he will beg his father's forgiveness instead. The father will forgive him, but lets him know the next time the son disobeys he will be punished. There is a time for forgiveness, as there is a time for the law to be implemented. The law is not forgiving, nor is it a respecter of persons. The law without mercy or favor from our God is costly and painful to us. We find in Scripture the most beloved thing in God's endless space is His Son. Yeshua was not tainted with His own sin. He was made unclean from the sins of mankind. All the same, sin is sin in the eyes of God and it must be punished. The ultimate punishment for sin is death.

Shaul says in **Romans 6:14** *"sin shall not be master over you,"* which means sin will no longer control you. When sin no longer has control, you have the power by the grace of God, to keep the Torah. How are you doing this? You are being justified, or being made righteous, by the law through grace which is Yeshua, as we just read in **Titus 3:7.** By grace, by the power of God, one keeps God's commandments. Yeshua is the mediator between man and the wrath of God. When a law is broken, condemnation is the result. If you don't break the law, you are not condemned by the law.

If you never murder anyone, you are not under the law that prohibits murder. But if you do murder someone and are caught, you then are under the law concerning murder. The understanding here is, "being under the law" concerns condemnation as a result of breaking the law. If you don't break it, you are not under the law. This is the same concept of driving the speed limit. You may pass by many police officers tracking your speed, but none of them are a threat to you if you are within the speed limits. You have no fear of them, because you are not breaking the law.

The Biblical definition of a wicked person is found in **Psalm 119:155 KJV,** *"Salvation is far from the wicked, for they do not seek Thy statutes [laws]."*

> . . .because through Christ Jesus the law of the Spirit who gives life has set you free from the law of sin and death. For what the law was powerless to do because it was weakened by the flesh, God did by sending his own Son in the likeness of sinful flesh to be a sin offering. And so he condemned sin in the flesh, in order that the righteous requirement of the law might be fully met in us, who do not live according to the flesh but according to the Spirit (**Romans 8:2-4 NIV**).

Does being set free from the law of sin and of death mean the commandments of God are no longer in effect? The Scriptures are specific that the Torah will be in effect forever, throughout all eternity. We also know that God's Word does not contradict itself. If we can agree on those two points, then the phrase "being set free from the law of sin and of death" cannot possibly mean the abolishment of the Torah. It means that if a person avoids sinning, he or she is free from the condemnation of the law that demands death for sin.

If the Torah defines righteousness and the righteousness of the law is being fulfilled in us, then we are not breaking any of God's commandments. Yeshua as a human being fulfilled the law in obedience to His Father. In **John 8:29,** *"The one who sent me is with me; he has not left me alone, for I always do what pleases him."* Yeshua makes it clear He always does the will of His Father, those things which are pleasing to Him. Yeshua has shown all human beings that we are not above keeping the laws of God and more importantly, that the Torah was relevant then and is relevant to us now.

Galatians, like Romans, has a lot to say about being justified.

> *Knowing that a man is not justified by the works of the law, but by the faith of Jesus Christ (Yeshua) even we have believed in Christ, that we might be justified by the faith of Jesus, and not by the works of the law: for by the works of the law shall no flesh be justified* (**Galatians 2:16 KJV**).

The law does not justify anyone. It condemns those who do not adhere to it. It is Yeshua who justifies on the judgment day, some to everlasting life and others to everlasting separation from God in the fire of God.

> *Multitudes who sleep in the dust of the earth will awake: some to everlasting life, others to shame and everlasting contempt (**Daniel 12:2 KJV**).*

Remember, being justified means being made righteous and being righteous is keeping God's commandments. God's grace is the power given to those who really want to obey Him. We see in these verses also that we are justified by faith. We are made righteous by faith in God's directions and instructions. Faith, therefore, operates like God's grace to give us the ability, the power and the fuel to obey God's law. This is why Shaul says that *"by the works of the law shall no flesh be justified,"* because nobody can obey the law without God's help.

> *If, while we seek to be justified in Christ, it becomes evident that we ourselves are sinners, does that mean that Christ promotes sin? Absolutely not! If I rebuild what I destroyed, I*

*prove that I am a lawbreaker. For through the law I died to the law so that I might live for God (**Galatians 2:17-19 NIV**).*

If we are dead to the Ten Commandments and the Torah, then we no longer need to obey the Torah. Are we free to commit murder or adultery, or any of the other sins prohibited in God's commandments? Consider that even the secular nations abide by the majority of the Ten Commandments. Notice how Shaul became dead to the law, through the law. The Torah convicted Shaul of sin, and by the grace of Yeshua he was able to overcome sin so that he no longer was under the condemnation of the law. If he never breaks the law, then he does not have to worry about the law. His character has become as that of Yeshua to the point that he naturally does not want to sin. He is dead to the law. He is born of God, according to **1 John 3:9 NIV**, *"No one who is born of God will continue to sin, because God's seed [Torah] remains in him; he cannot go on sinning, because he has been born of God."*

1 John 3:9 is reminiscent of **Galatians 3:24-25 KJV**, *"Wherefore the law was our schoolmaster to bring us to Christ, that we might be justified by faith. But after that faith is come, we are no longer under a schoolmaster."* How is it the Torah is our schoolmaster? The law points out our sins as Shaul illuminates in **Romans 7:7 NIV**:

"What shall we say, then? Is the law sin? Certainly not! Indeed I would not have known what sin was except through the law. For I would not have known what coveting really was if the law had not said, 'Do not covet.'"

When we look into the laws of God and compare our characters to that law, we realize that we are in a terrible condition. When faith comes, the power of Christ allows us to overcome sin and obey the law. We are then able to quit sinning. When this happens, we no longer need the schoolmaster, for our characters are then in harmony with Christ.

*I do not frustrate the grace of God: for if righteousness come by the law, then Christ is dead in vain (**Galatians 2:21 NIV**).*

The power of Yeshua's grace enables us to obey the law. Shaul, therefore, must be obeying the Ten Commandments and all the Torah. When he says that righteousness does not come by the law (of sacrifice), he is saying that he cannot keep the law by himself without grace. Shaul is also saying here that if he could keep the law without Christ (by sacrificing), then Christ died in vain.

> *O foolish Galatians, who hath bewitched you, that ye should not obey the truth, before whose eyes Jesus Christ hath been evidently set forth, crucified among you?* (**Galatians 3:1 KJV**)

Consider the phrase "obey the truth." What is this truth Shaul is referring to?

> *Thou art near, O LORD;* **and all thy commandments are truth** *(Psalm 119:151 KJV).*

Shaul's reference to someone bewitching the Galatians is about teaching them that they no longer needed to obey the rest of God's commandments. Those who receive God's Holy Spirit are those who are obedient to God and to His Torah.

> *And we are his witnesses of these things; and so is also the Holy Ghost, whom God hath given to them that obey him* (**Acts 5:32 KJV**).

Those who disregard and do not obey the commandments of God cannot receive the Holy Spirit. It is impossible for us to obey the law without faith and the grace of Yeshua. We cannot receive the Spirit by trying to obey the law without Yeshua's help. Therefore we must have faith and obtain grace to give us the power to obey the law so we can receive God's Holy Spirit.

> *Are ye so foolish? Having begun in the Spirit, are ye now made perfect by the flesh? Have ye suffered so many things in vain? if it be yet in vain. He therefore that ministereth to you the Spirit, and worketh miracles among you, doeth*

he it by the works of the law, or by the hearing of faith?
*(**Galatians 3:3-5 KJV**).*

The Galatians became self-confident, believing they could keep
the law of their own accord without the grace (help) of Christ. Of
course they could not keep the law without grace, so when they
became proud and self-sufficient, they became sinners.

Even as Abraham believed God, and it was accounted to him
*for righteousness. (**Galatians 3:6 KJV**).*

And this I say, that the covenant, that was confirmed before
of God in Christ, the law, which was four hundred and thirty
years after, cannot disannul, that it should make the promise
of none effect. For if the inheritance be of the law, it is no
more of promise: but God gave it to Abraham by promise.
Wherefore then serveth the law? It was added because of
transgressions, till the seed should come to whom the promise
was made; and it was ordained by angels in the hand of a
mediator. Now a mediator is not a mediator of one, but God
*is one (**Galatians 3:17-20**).*

These verses speak of a law that was added four hundred and
thirty years after the covenant God made with Abraham. These
verses also tell us why the law was added, because of transgression.
We have already seen that transgression or sin is **breaking any of**
the commandments. No law equals no transgression. We also saw
the commandments existed long before the earth was created.

He is subject to guardians and trustees until the time set
by his father. So also, when we were children, we were in
slavery under the basic principles of the world. But when
the time had fully come, God sent his Son, born of a woman,
born under law, to redeem those under law, that we might
receive the full rights of sons. Because you are sons, God
sent the Spirit of his Son into our hearts, the Spirit who calls
out, "Abba, Father." So you are no longer a slave, but a

*son; and since you are a son, God has made you also an heir (**Galatians 4:2-7 NIV**).*

Shaul mentions that God sent His Son, born under the law so that we might receive the full rights of sons. Since we are sons, we can now call him Father. Yeshua was born under the law for God to give us the rights of a son. This Scripture tells us that God wants us to live by His law just as His Son was born under the law.

THE ORDINANCES

*Blotting out the handwriting of ordinances that was against us, which were against us, and took it out of the way, nailing it to his cross; And having spoiled principalities and powers, he made a show of them openly, triumphing over them in it. Let no man therefore judge you in meat, or in drink, or in respect of a holyday, or of the new moon, or of the Sabbath days: Which are a shadow of things to come; but the body is of Christ (**Colossians 2:14-17 KJV**).*

We are encouraged to obey Adonai despite the ridicule or judgment we may receive for eating kosher foods or drinking wine on special holy days, following Jewish festivals, Passover, Feast of Trumpets, Rosh-Chodesh, or the Shabbat. The Torah contains four different types of laws. In Colossians it reads *the handwritten ordinances were against us and nailed to the cross.* We must determine which laws (ordinances) were against us, as the Scripture says, and which are forever. The laws that continually stated they were forever cannot be the handwriting of ordinances, which were against us that Yeshua fulfilled on the cross.

The Ten Commandments are definitely not against us, for by observance of them the universe is guaranteed peace and happiness. If everyone on earth kept the Ten Commandments perfectly the world would be a much better place to live. There would be no wars or strife. Everyone would deal honestly and with integrity with his neighbor. The health laws are not against us, they are there to protect us from disease and poor health. They teach us proper hygiene. The civil laws are not against us, as there needs to be just and proper discipline and punishment for those who intentionally or unintentionally break the laws. These laws cannot be against us either.

This leaves us with the ordinances pertaining to animal sacrifices. Yeshua's sacrifice satisfied the eternal need for a pure sacrifice therefore animal sacrifices ceased.

> *And he shall confirm the covenant with many for one week: and in the midst of the week he shall cause the sacrifice and the oblation to cease. . . . (**Daniel 9:27 KJV**).*

These animal sacrifices were part of the ceremonial laws. Therefore what Christ nailed to the cross were these ceremonial laws dealing with animal sacrifices.

> *And having spoiled principalities and powers, he made a show of them openly, triumphing over them in it. Let no man therefore judge you in meat, or in drink, or in respect of an holyday, or of the new moon, or of the Sabbath days: Which are a shadow of things to come; but the body is of Christ (**Colossians 2:15-17 KJV**).*

Shaul is addressing the Jewish believers in Yeshua concerning the ridicule received for practicing the Jewish laws. Shaul is admonishing them not to let people judge them for practicing their Jewish faith, as they are ordained in God's laws:

> *You observe days, and months, and times, and years. (**Galatians 4:10 KJV**).*

Yeshua was from the beginning, He was the word of God (Torah), He was the Word of God made flesh and He said our love for Him would be shown in keeping his commandments. He fulfilled the promises and prophecies foretold about Him. It was men who rejected the law of God (Yeshua) and nailed Him to the tree. Yet Yeshua's death did not deny or negate the law. His death fulfilled the law and provided the way for us to keep His commandments. He said if you love, me keep my commandments

Yeshua's death effectively nailed the ordinances or the regulations concerning sacrifices to His cross. It was the sacrifices that were against us. The demand for the life of the person who sins (substituted by the sacrifice of a kosher animal) is what was against us. It is by grace, a gift from God, that Yeshua came to give his life and die for our sins.

Crucifixion with nails was uncommon even in Roman times. Usually ropes were used to bind the prisoner to the cross (much like they did for thousands of years when sacrificing animals) along with the verdict against the prisoner. But the Romans nailed Yeshua to the cross rather than tying him with a rope to expedite His death because of the great Shabbat (a double Shabbat, the regular seven day Shabbat and the Passover), however a higher force was at work. God required Him to be nailed because he was the ordinance nailed to his cross, the ultimate sacrifice, so that all would be fulfilled.

Laws defining righteous behavior given to Israel were known and observed long before the covenant at Sinai was made. Both Shaul and the disciples continued to sacrifice after the death and resurrection of Yeshua. The reason for this is the sacrifices were only relevant to the temple. After the destruction of the temple in 70 AD, the people who believed in Yeshua as their covering for sin would not need to sacrifice any longer. The temple being destroyed in 70 AD is significant. Seven is the number of completion and ten is the number for righteousness. The perfect sacrifice, Yeshua (ten), completed (seven) the need for animal sacrifices (10x7=70), so 70 AD was when the temple sacrifices had to cease.

> *Take heed to thyself that thou offer not thy burnt offerings in every place that thou seest: But in the place which the LORD shall choose in one of thy tribes, there thou shalt offer thy burnt offerings, and there thou shalt do all that I command thee (**Deuteronomy 12:13-14**).*

There is no place for the Jewish people to sacrifice with the destruction of the temple. The sacrifices were connected and relevant only to the temple, the house of God. As soon as the temple was destroyed, all the relevant laws including sacrifices had to cease. In the last days, there will be a temporary structure built (tent) whereby the Jewish people will resume sacrifices, but it will not pertain to the believers in Yeshua as He fulfilled these ordinances.

ONE LAW TWO PEOPLE

*For I think that God hath set forth us the apostles last, as it were appointed to death: **for we are made a spectacle unto the world, and to angels, and to men (1 Corinthians 4:9 KJV)**.*

*T*he word *spectacle* is translated from the Greek word *theatron*, which means "theater." As God's creation, we were created to demonstrate what happens when a society disobeys His laws. The drama that unfolds on earth is the final result of man breaking God's commandments. Many blame God for the suffering in this world. The Torah has been given to us as a protection against actions that cause us pain, sickness and an untimely death. It was written so that we know how to obtain a good life, health and a relationship with our Creator. It is also written as a warning of what will happen if we disobey and go against the will of God. There are consequences of pain, sickness and death for disobedient. With all of this information we still disobey, suffer and then blame God.

The wars, trouble, pain and suffering all over the earth today are a direct result of people disregarding God's commandments. Misery, pain and death are the natural consequences of disregarding the Torah of God. Without obeying God's law there can be no shalom, health, or life.

*The earth dries up and withers, the world languishes and withers, the exalted of the earth languish. The earth is defiled by its people; **they have disobeyed the laws, violated the statutes and broken the everlasting covenant.** Therefore a curse consumes the earth; its people must bear their guilt. Therefore earth's inhabitants are burned up, and very few are left (**Isaiah 24:4-6 NIV**).*

The earth is defiled because of the sin of mankind. We are cursed as a result and bear the guilt and consequences of disobedience to God's Torah. Why is a prophecy that is being fulfilled today saying we "have disobeyed the laws, violated the statutes and broken the everlasting covenant", if the law was done away with as so many presume Shaul to be saying?

*"As the new heavens and the new earth that I make will endure before me," declares the LORD, "so will your name and descendants endure. **From one new moon to another and from one Sabbath to another, all mankind will come and bow down before me,"** says the LORD. "And they will go out and look upon the dead bodies of those who rebelled against me; their worm will not die, nor will their fire be quenched, and they will be loathsome to all mankind" (**Isaiah 66:22-24 NIV**).*

Isaiah 66 shows us that the laws related to the Shabbat and new moon will still be in force in the future kingdom. Why is it we think Shaul is telling us the law is no longer required, yet Yeshua's reign on earth will include observance of the Torah? Those who say the laws of God are somehow changed or passed away seem to miss the point that the Bible was given to direct us on how to relate to God as well as man. It is a fence to protect us from harm and to keep us from harming others. More importantly, the laws of God keep order in the universe if obeyed as intended:

*What shall we say, then? Shall we go on sinning so that grace may increase? By no means! We died to sin; how can we live in it any longer? (**Romans 6:1-2 NIV**)*

What is sin? How is someone to know what sin is if he has no guidelines, namely the (law) Torah? Torah specifies what sin is. The New Testament still speaks of sin, as does Shaul after the death of Yeshua. The Bible provides us with the platform to create harmonious relationships with our fellow human beings on earth, as well as insight into having a relationship with our Father in heaven. More importantly, it allows us to learn about and identify sin.

Adam and Chaya (Eve) may have lived for hundreds or thousands of years in the garden without sin because there was no law. But as soon as the command was given to not eat the fruit from a certain tree, the opportunity came for disobedience and for sin to exist. The very law that was given to man is also the law that brought in sin when it was broken. The law is also the only thing that can point out sin, and if obeyed, can protect us to from wrong choice and ultimately please Adonai.

When Yeshua drank wine and broke bread at the Last Supper, He was doing what Jews do every time they perform the Kiddush ceremony before a festival or Shabbat meal. When Yeshua began His prayers with, "Our Father, which art in heaven," He was following the pattern of prayers used by the Perushim (Pharisees), which still form part of the Jewish Daily Prayer Book.

When Yeshua spoke in parables as he did in the Gospels, He was using expressions familiar to any student of the Talmudic writings. Shaul taught in that same fashion:

*Paul, (**Shaul**) a servant of Jesus Christ, called to be an apostle, separated unto the gospel of God, [which he had promised afore by his prophets in the holy Scriptures] concerning his Son Jesus Christ our Lord, which was made of the seed of David according to the flesh; And declared to be the Son of God with power, according to the spirit of holiness, by the resurrection from the dead: By whom we have received grace and apostleship, for obedience to the faith* *among all nations, for his name: Among whom are ye also the called of Jesus Christ: To all that be in Rome, beloved of God, called to be saints: Grace to you and peace from God our Father, and the Lord Jesus Christ. First, I thank my God through Jesus Christ for you all, that your faith is spoken of throughout the whole world (**Romans 1:1-8 KJV**).*

The spirit of truth was the force driving Shaul to tell the world about the Jewish Messiah. He started the book of Romans with acknowledging that he surrendered himself as a servant to his Master Yeshua. Shaul's declaration of surrender to Yeshua is a confession that His allegiance and loyalty changed from the teachings of the rabbis to the teachings of Yeshua, who is the word of GOD; the Torah manifested in human form. Shaul points out the validity of the Old Testament Scriptures from the prophets and the Writings regarding the coming Mashiach:

*Paul, a prisoner of Christ Jesus, and Timothy our brother, To Philemon our dear friend and fellow worker (**Philemon 1:1 NIV**).*

*For this reason I, Paul, the prisoner of Christ Jesus for the sake of you Gentiles (**Ephesians 3:1 NIV**).*

*But now the righteousness of God without the law is manifested, being witnessed by the law and the prophets; Even the righteousness of God which is by faith of Yeshua Ha'Mashiach unto all and upon all them that believe: for there is no difference: For all have sinned, and come short of the glory of God; Being justified freely by his grace through the redemption that is in Mashiach Yeshua: (**Romans 3:21-24 KJV**)*

If disobedience to God's laws removes us from God, then obedience to God's law brings reconciliation and salvation.

*The same laws and regulations will apply both to you and to the alien living among you (**Numbers 15:16 NIV**).*

*The same law applies to the native-born and to the alien living among you (**Exodus 12:49 NIV**).*

Unfortunately, many will take one or two misunderstood verses of Shaul's writings and presume he is challenging the authority of Yeshua. Shaul, who never saw Yeshua and never studied with Yeshua, came to the conclusion that Yeshua was the Messiah from his knowledge of the Torah and previous studies.

- All the Torah that was written by Moshe in the presence of God
- All the prophets
- All the writings of David and Solomon
- All the writers of the Gospels, which recorded the words spoken by Yeshua, the author of the Torah. The one who claimed ownership of the commandments when he said, "If you love me, keep My commandments."

Do not think that I have come to abolish the law or the prophets; I have not come to abolish them but to fulfill them. **I tell you the truth, until heaven and earth disappear, not the smallest letter, not the least stroke of a pen, will by any means disappear from the law until everything is accomplished.** *Anyone who breaks one of the least of these commandments and teaches others to do the same will be called least in the kingdom of heaven, but whoever practices and teaches these commands will be called great in the kingdom of heaven. For I tell you that unless your righteousness surpasses that of the Pharisees and the teachers of the law, you will certainly not enter the kingdom of heaven (**Matthew 5:17-20 NIV**).*

*So then, **the law is holy**, and the commandment is holy, righteous and good (**Romans 7:12 NIV**).*

It is the law that is the arbiter of what is righteous and what is unrighteous. How can anyone think Shaul is throwing out the law when he is still writing and exhorting about righteousness and holiness? On the surface, **Romans 3:21-24** (above) appears to contradict the supremacy of the Torah. Shaul seems to state that we cannot attain righteousness on our own.

In effect, he is echoing **Ecclesiastes 7:20 NASB**, which states, *"Indeed, there is not a righteous man on earth who continually does good and who never sins."* Are we missing something here? If there is no Tzadikim (righteous), why does the Torah call Hanoch, Noah, Job, Avraham, Yitzhak and Ya'acov, Daniel righteous? Is righteousness found in the New Testament only? Is it found only after the death and resurrection of Yeshua? Not according to Ya'acov.

> *And the Scripture was fulfilled which saith, Abraham believed God, and it was imputed unto him for righteousness: and he was called the Friend of God (**James 2:23 KJV**).*

Ezekiel 14:14 upholds the righteousness of other men, as well:

> *Though these three men, **Noah, Daniel and Job**, were in it, they should deliver but their own souls by their righteousness, saith the Lord GOD (**Ezekiel 14:14 KJV**).*

The sages always understood that a person can be righteous, but not completely righteous, which is still in alignment with the previous verses as well as what Shaul has written. There are no contradictions. The Torah clearly states:

> *Follow [**pursue**] justice and justice alone, so that you may live and possess the land the LORD your God is giving you (**Deuteronomy 16:20 NIV**).*

We are to continue to follow or pursue perfect righteousness (justice), even though we know we will sometimes fail. That is why Yeshua came. He brings grace to us in our failures. He brings true justice to us, not as men perceive it should be, but according to the intent of our heart, whether to please God or to defy Him.

> *So then, my beloved, just as you have always obeyed, not as in my presence only, but now much more in my absence, work out your salvation with fear and trembling; for it is God who works in you to will and to act in order to fulfill his good purpose (**Philippians 2:12,13 NASB**).*

> *Because it is written, "Be ye holy; for I am holy" (**1 Peter 1:16 KJV**).*

Both Shaul and Shimon's statements were taken from the book of Leviticus, just as all of their other statements and teachings originated from the Tanakh. Shaul is telling the Gentiles to labor in obedience in the Word, in the Torah, the only book available with instructions concerning salvation.

In **Philippians 2:12,** the Greek word for *work* is *katergazomai*. It translates as "working to completion." We are to work to complete the demands of the Torah. Through Yeshua, God works in us to give us the will to do what needs to be done to bring forth salvation ourselves. Shaul said we are to work out our own salvation with fear and trembling; that means to study the Scriptures and become wise through application.

Shaul wanted his readers to understand that he would not always be with them. He was going away and they were going to be on their own with the Word of God (Torah). They must soon work without his leadership, totally relying on the Torah as their guide. Shaul's letters never expressed anything new. His writings were never about encouraging them to seek another way for salvation. He is telling them that salvation can only be found and obtained in the Torah.

The same truth was revealed to Abraham in Genesis:

> *. . .because Abraham obeyed me and kept my requirements, my commands, my decrees and my laws (**Genesis 26:5 NIV**).*

It was Avraham's righteousness that earned the title "friend of God."

> *And the Scripture was fulfilled that says, "Abraham believed God, and it was credited to him as righteousness," and he was called God's friend. (James 2:23 NIV).*

It was the same Torah Hanoch kept that earned him salvation from death.

> *Enoch (Hanoch) walked with God; then he was no more, because God took him away (Genesis 5:24 NIV).*

The same Torah Eliyahu (Elijah) kept that earned him salvation from death and corruption.

> *As they were walking along and talking together, suddenly a chariot of fire and horses of fire appeared and separated the two of them, and Elijah went up to heaven in a whirlwind (2 Kings 2:11 NIV).*

It was the same Torah that is commanded unto us for a relationship and salvation.

Shaul's portion of Scripture from **Philippians 2:12-13** is similar to the farewell speech of Moshe when he addressed Israel in **Deuteronomy 1:1-4:19**. Just before they were to cross over the river Jordan, Moshe tells Israel, that he would no longer be with them. They had to rely on their past experiences on God, but mostly they had to depend on the Torah to allow them to enter the Promise Land and find salvation. As Israel crossed the river Jordan, their future and prosperity was dependent on adhering to the warning of Moshe's farewell speech. The Levites crossed ahead of the nation in order to write the Torah commandments on the mountain rocks for the nation to see. They read aloud the blessings awaiting those who obey and the curses for those who reject the Laws of Adonai.

GOD DOES NOT CHANGE

*I the LORD do not change. So you, O descendants of Jacob, are not destroyed (**Malachi 3:6 NIV**).*

*M*alachi represents the last of God's word to mankind until the time of Yeshua, a gap of four hundred years. The process for relationship and salvation remains the same from the days of Adam, Hanoch (Enoch), Noah, Avraham and Moshe all the way until the final judgment day.

> *Then (**Shimon**) Peter opened his mouth, and said, "Of a truth I perceive that God is no respecter of persons: But in every nation he that feareth him, and worketh righteousness, is accepted with him" (**Acts 10:34-35 KJV**).*

Shaul recorded Shimon's (Peter's) words because they convey a very important message—the uniformity, or standard of God's Torah throughout the world and to all the people. Yeshua's death was universal; He had to die for the entire world—not just the Jews and not just the Gentiles.

The need of the Torah and Yeshua's sacrifice points to the fact that every person must be obedient to God. No one is exempted from God's demands.

*Men and brethren, children of the stock of Abraham, and
whosoever among you feareth God, to you is the word of this
salvation sent (**Acts 13:26 KJV**).*

One can hold a Torah scroll written only a few days ago and one
written two thousand years ago and find that they are the same in
style in spacing and in the pigment of the dye. The uniformity of the
Torah was reflected in the teaching of the disciples. While having
their own style of teaching, the content had to be the same. The
door for relationship and salvation is opened not only for the Jew
from the stock of Avraham, but for all people and nations who are
willing to enter into the covenant God made with Avraham, Yitzhak
and Ya'acov.

*There is **one body**, and **one Spirit**, even as ye are called in
one hope of your calling; **One Lord, one faith, one baptism,
One God and Father of all**, who is above all, and through
all, and in you all (**Ephesians 4:4-6 KJV**).*

The uniformity of the Torah today also indicates God's preserva-
tion of His Word in such a manner that we can trust it to study and
apply to our lives. Not only has God's people done a remarkable job
of preserving the antiquity of the Torah and its oral traditions, but
they have kept track of the times and seasons. The Shabbat and holy
days that we keep today are exactly as they have always been.

The Bible and its authors, along with archaeological discoveries
and other sacred texts give evidence that there are no substantial
changes in our copies of the Scriptures today.

Consider the following:

•   God promises to preserve His Word that it will never be far
    from His people, nor will it vanish.

*As the rain and the snow come down from heaven, and do
not return to it without watering the earth and making it bud
and flourish, so that it yields seed for the sower and bread*

for the eater, so is my word that goes out from my mouth: It will not return to me empty, but will accomplish what I desire and achieve the purpose for which I sent it **(Isaiah 55:10-11 NIV).**

"As for me, this is my covenant with them," says the Lord. "My Spirit, who is on you, will not depart from you, and my words that I have put in your mouth will always be on your lips, on the lips of your children and on the lips of their descendants—from this time on and forever," says the Lord **(Isaiah 59:21 NIV).**

- Yeshua's word to us is the word of God and will not pass away as long as heaven and earth are here.

Heaven and earth will pass away, but my words will never pass away **(Matthew 24:35 NIV).**

- Shimon (Peter), to whom Yeshua gave the keys of authority to in all matters relating to the Torah, also affirms the ever-lasting and ever-present nature of God's Word:

For, "All people are like grass, and all their glory is like the flowers of the field; the grass withers and the flowers fall, but the word of the Lord endures forever." And this is the word that was preached to you **(1 Peter 1:24-25 NIV).**

- Around 400 BC, the Torah was translated into Greek (the Septuagint).
- The Dead Sea Scrolls dates from around 100 BC to after the time of Christ and we can compare them with our Bibles today. The Dead Sea scrolls are composed of some ninety-five thousand fragments from over eight hundred manuscripts of the Bible and other related writings. A third of the Dead Sea Scrolls are related to the Old Testament.
- The Targums (the Aramaic translation of the Hebrew Bible) were written about the time of Yeshua.

- Forty different authors wrote the Old Testament across sixty generations and sixty-six manuscripts. These authors wrote the Old Testament and were able to write content that was uniform and in harmony between each other.
- The verifiable and ongoing foresight and fulfillment of Biblical prophesy.

FEAR AND HOLINESS

*For I am the LORD your God: ye shall therefore sanctify yourselves, and ye shall **be holy; for I am holy:** neither shall ye defile yourselves with any manner of creeping thing that creepeth upon the earth. For I am the LORD that bringeth you up out of the land of Egypt, to be your God: ye shall therefore **be holy, for I am holy** (Leviticus 11:44-45 KJV).*

The essence of holiness is being set apart, being different. Holiness is accomplished through obedience to the Torah. When we live in obedience to God's law sets us apart from the rest of the world and makes us holy. How will God know His people if there is no difference in their actions from those who do not believe and follow the law? Maintaining fear of the Lord is not a part-time thing, nor is it for the Jew only. It is for all who seek relationship and salvation with the one and true God of the universe.

Now these are the commandments, the statutes, and the judgments, which the LORD your God commanded to teach you, that ye might do them in the land whither ye go to possess it: That thou might fear the LORD thy God, to keep all his statutes and his commandments, which I command thee, thou, and thy son, and thy son's son, all the days of *thy life; and that thy days may be prolonged (**Deuteronomy 6:1-2 KJV**).*

*One law shall be to him that is home born, and unto the stranger that sojourneth among you (**Exodus 12:49 KJV**).*

Shaul is referring to Exodus 12:49 when he writes:

*There is neither Jew nor Greek, there is neither bond nor free, there is neither male nor female: for ye are all one in Mashiach Yeshua (**Galatians 3:28 KJV**).*

When writing his letters to the churches, Shaul is using the Tanakh to arrive at his conclusions. As a rabbi, he could not introduce new doctrine. He could only expound on the Torah. A severe warning awaited those who wavered from orthodox teaching as found in the Torah and also echoed in Revelation.

*If a prophet, or one who foretells by dreams, appears among you and announces to you a miraculous sign or wonder, and if the sign or wonder of which he has spoken takes place, and he says, "Let us follow other gods (gods you have not known) and let us worship them," you must not listen to the words of that prophet or dreamer. The LORD your God is testing you to find out whether you love him with all your heart and with all your soul. It is the LORD your God you must follow, and him you must revere. Keep his commands and obey him; serve him and hold fast to him. That **prophet or dreamer must be put to death,** because he preached rebellion against the LORD your God, who brought you out of Egypt and redeemed you from the land of slavery; he has tried to turn you from the way the LORD your God commanded you to follow. You must purge the evil from among you (**Deuteronomy 13:1-5 NIV**).*

And if anyone takes words away from this book of prophecy, God will take away from him his share in the tree of life and *in the holy city, which are described in this book (**Revelation 22:19 NIV**).*

The Hebrew context for fear is one of respect, honor and obedience. From everlasting to everlasting speaks of people from the beginning—long before there were Jews.

The same principles for relationship existed in the Garden when God gave a specific command to Adam before the Jewish people were established. God told Adam that he was not to eat the fruit of the forbidden tree; more importantly, there was a consequence for eating the fruit Adonai forbade. It was death. God's command to Adam was not an issue of ethnicity, color, or tribal sect. The command was for the human race to practice obedience to their Creator. This sets the pattern for every law of God that came after the fall of Adam. This is the importance of understanding the fear the Lord.

> *The LORD commanded us to obey all these decrees and to fear the LORD our God, so that we might always prosper and be kept alive, as is the case today (**Deuteronomy 6:24 NIV**).*

> *But be sure to fear the LORD and serve him faithfully with all your heart; consider what great things he has done for you. Yet if you persist in doing evil, both you and your king will be swept away (**1 Samuel 12:24-25 NIV**).*

> *Behold, the eye of the LORD is upon them that fear him, upon them that hope in his mercy; (**Psalm 33:18 KJV**)*

> *O fear the LORD, ye his saints: for there is no lack to them that fear him (**Psalm 34:9 KJV**).*

> *For thou, O God, hast heard my vows: thou hast given me the heritage of those that fear thy name (**Psalm 61:5 ASV**).*

> *But the mercy of the LORD is from everlasting to everlasting upon them that fear him, and his righteousness unto children's children; (**Psalm 103:17 KJV**)*

*Serve the LORD with fear and rejoice with trembling. Kiss the Son, lest he be angry and you be destroyed in your way, for his wrath can flare up in a moment. Blessed are all who take refuge in him (**Psalm 2:11-12 NIV**).*

Kiss the son speaks of appeasement; it is a reflection of what all Jews do when they enter a dwelling or exit a dwelling. They kiss the **mezuzah**, a case mounted to the doorframe with a parchment with **Deuteronomy 6:4-9** that says, *"Hear, O Israel: The LORD our God, the LORD is one"* written on it. They also kiss the **Tzitzit**, the fringes of the tallit. Like the mezuzah, the tallit represents Yeshua the Messiah. The tallit has knots that represent the six hundred and thirteen commandments (6+1+3=10, the number of righteousness and judgment). Kissing the mezuzah and the tallit is like a man who kisses his wife with deep love and affection.

The theme of these Scriptures is fear the Lord and walk in obedience to the Lord.

*Come, ye children, hearken unto me: I will teach you the **fear** of the LORD. What man is he that **desireth life, and loveth many days, that he may see good**? Keep thy tongue from evil, and thy lips from speaking guile. **Depart from evil**, and **do good**; seek peace, and pursue it. The eyes of the LORD are **upon the righteous**, and his ears are open unto their cry. The face of the **LORD is against them that do evil, to cut off the remembrance of them from the earth** (Psalm 34:11-16 KJV).*

God contrasts those who fear the Lord with the wicked that have no fear of God and transgress without concern for the consequences. Why do Christians as a whole turn away from the commandments of the very Lord they confess to and believe in? The answer is in Timothy. Their conscience is seared:

*Such teachings come through hypocritical liars, whose **consciences have been seared** as with a hot iron (**1 Timothy 4:2 NIV**).*

A seared conscience means that your senses are dulled to God's Word and His commands. That is when fear of the Lord has been lost. It's like having scar tissue on your body where the nerves have been damaged resulting in a loss of feeling. The nerves have been severed and no communication gets through between the affected area and the brain. It is dead.

Shaul's ministry was with pagans and he was able to win thousands of them into the light of the Torah. Shaul exhorted the Philippians to fear the Lord so they would obey God when he (Shaul) was not present.

> *Now the Bereans were of more noble character than the Thessalonians, for they received the message with great eagerness and examined the Scriptures every day to see if what Paul said was true (**Acts 17:10-11 NIV**).*

Shaul spent his entire adult life in teaching the Torah to unbelievers. His mission was to unite the teachings of the Jews to those who are being grafted into the covenant of the patriarchs so these new converts would be unified.

> *As also in all his epistles, speaking in them of these things; in which are some things hard to be understood, which they that are unlearned and unstable wrest, as they do also the other Scriptures, unto their own destruction. (**2 Peter 3:16 KJV**).*

> ***The transgression of the wicked** saith within my heart, that there is no fear of God before his eyes (**Psalm 36:1 KJV**).*

> *God shall hear, and **afflict them**, even he that abideth of old. Selah. Because they have no changes **therefore they fear not God (Psalm 55:19 KJV**).*

> *Destruction and misery are in their ways: And the way of peace have they not known: **There is no fear of God before their eyes (Romans 3:16-18 KJV**).*

*And the LORD spoke to Moses, saying, "Speak to all the congregation of the children of Israel, and say to them: 'You shall be holy, for I the LORD your God am holy.' Every one of you shall revere his mother and his father, and keep My Sabbaths: I am the LORD your God (**Leviticus 19:1-3 AKJ**).*

God tells Moshe to be holy because He (God) is holy. He loves us so much and He wants us, the people of His creation, to be holy just as He is holy. The only way to achieve holiness is through keeping His Shabbats and honoring our parents.

*Do your best to present yourself to God as one approved, a workman who does not need to be ashamed and who correctly handles the word of truth (**2 Timothy 2:15 NIV**).*

QUESTIONS & ANSWERS

QUESTION:

*I*f God's people are keeping the Ten Commandments, what will happen to them?

ANSWER:

They will have to defend themselves.

> *Then the dragon was enraged at the woman and went off to wage war against the rest of her offspring—those who keep God's commands and hold fast their testimony about Jesus* (**Revelation 12:17 NIV**).

They will be banned from worship and killed:

> *They will put you out of the synagogue; in fact, the time is coming when anyone who kills you will think they are offering a service to God* (**John 16:2 NIV**).

They will be persecuted:

> *In fact, everyone who wants to live a godly life in Christ Jesus will be persecuted. . . (**2 Timothy 3:12 NIV**).*

QUESTION:

What qualities will God's people have?

ANSWER:

They keep the Shabbat.

> *Therefore, since the promise of entering his rest still stands, let us be careful that none of you be found to have fallen short of it. For we also have had the good news proclaimed to us, just as they did; but the message they heard was of no value to them, because they did not share the faith of those who obeyed. Now we who have believed enter that rest, just as God has said, "So I declared on oath in my anger, 'They shall never enter my rest.' And yet his works have been finished since the creation of the world. For somewhere he has spoken about the seventh day in these words: "On the seventh day God rested from all his works." And again in the passage above he says, "They shall never enter my rest." Therefore since it still remains for some to enter that rest, and since those who formerly had the good news proclaimed to them did not go in because of their disobedience, God again set a certain day, calling it "Today." This he did when a long time later he spoke through David, as in the passage already quoted: "Today, if you hear his voice, do not harden your hearts." For if Joshua had given them rest, God would not have spoken later about another day. There remains, then, a Sabbath-rest for the people of God; for anyone who enters God's rest also rests from their works, just as God did from his. Let us, therefore, make every effort to enter that*

rest, so that no one will perish by following their example of disobedience (**Hebrews 4:1-11 NIV**).

They keep the commandments of God.

*This calls for patient endurance on the part of the people of God who keep his commands and remain faithful to Jesus (**Revelation 14:12 NIV**).*

*Blessed are those who wash their robes, that they may have the right to the tree of life and may go through the gates into the city (**Revelation 22:14 NIV**).*

QUESTION:

Why are God's people keeping the Ten Commandments?

ANSWER:

For they love God and Yeshua.

*If you love me, you will keep my commandments (**John 14:15 KJV**).*

*If you keep my commands, you will stay in my love- just as I have kept my Father's commands and stay in his love (**John 15:10 KJV**).*

*Here is how we know that we love God's children: when we love God, we also do what he commands. For loving God means obeying his commands. Moreover, his commands are not burdensome. . . (**1 John 5:2-3 KJV**).*

QUESTION:

Who will have the privilege of walking into the Great City?

ANSWER:

Those who are saved of the nations, the righteous who kept the commandments of Adonai.

> *The nations will walk by its light, and the kings of the earth will bring their splendor into it. On no day will its gates ever be shut, for there will be no night there. The glory and honor of the nations will be brought into it. **Nothing impure will ever enter it**, nor will anyone who does what is shameful or deceitful, but only **those whose names are written in the Lamb's book of life (Revelation 21:24-27 NIV).***

QUESTION:

Whose names are inscribed into the foundations of the City of God?

ANSWER:

The twelve apostles of Yeshua.

> *The wall of the city had twelve foundations, and on them were the names of **the twelve apostles of the Lamb (Revelation 21:14 NIV).***

QUESTION:

Whose names are inscribed above the gates of the City of God?

ANSWER:

The twelve tribes of Israel.

> *It had a great, high wall with twelve gates, and with twelve angels at the gates. On the gates were written the names of **the twelve tribes of Israel (Revelation 21:12 NIV).***

QUESTION:

What will Yeshua find when he returns?

ANSWER:

Corrupt men, Ungodly, lacking in true faith.

> *I tell you that he will avenge them speedily. Nevertheless when the Son of man cometh, **shall he find faith** on the earth? (**Luke 18:8 KJV**)*

> *This know also, that in the last days perilous times shall come. For men shall be lovers of their own selves, covetous, boasters, proud, blasphemers, disobedient to parents, unthankful, unholy, Without natural affection, trucebreakers, false accusers, incontinent, fierce, despisers of those that are good, Traitors, heady, high-minded, lovers of pleasures more than lovers of God; Having a **form of godliness**, but denying the power thereof: from such turn away. For of this sort are they which creep into houses, and lead captive silly women laden with sins, led away with divers lusts, **Ever learning, and never able to come to the knowledge of the truth.** Now as Jannes and Jambres withstood Moses, so do these also resist the truth: men of corrupt minds, reprobate concerning the faith (**2 Timothy 3:1-8 KVJ**).*

Iniquity abounding on earth.

> *And because **iniquity shall abound, the love of many shall wax cold (Matthew 24:12 KJV**).*

Deception:

> *Beware of false prophets, which come to you in sheep's clothing, **but inwardly they are ravening wolves (Matthew 7:15 KJV**).*

155

*And Yeshua answered and said unto them, Take heed that no man deceive you. For **many shall come in my name, saying, I am Christ; and shall deceive many** (Matthew 24:4-5 KJV).*

*Even as Sodom and Gomorrah, and the cities about them in like manner, **giving themselves over to fornication, and going after strange flesh**, are set forth for an example, suffering the vengeance of eternal fire. Likewise also these **filthy dreamers** defile the flesh, despise dominion, and speak evil of dignities (**Jude 1:7-8 KJV**).*

Chaos and turmoil:

*And ye shall **hear of wars and rumors of wars**: see that ye be not troubled: for all these things must come to pass, but the end is not yet. 7 For **nation shall rise against nation, and kingdom against kingdom**: and there shall be **famines, and pestilences, and earthquakes**, in divers places (**Matthew 24:6-7 KJV**).*

IN CLOSING

For the time will come when **men will not put up with sound doctrine**. *Instead, to suit their own desires, they will* **gather around them a great number of teachers to say what their itching ears want to hear.** *They* **will turn their ears away from the truth and turn aside to myths** *(2 Timothy 4:3-4 NIV).*

The wrath of God is being revealed from heaven against **all the godlessness and wickedness of men who suppress the truth by their wickedness,** *since what may be known about God is plain to them, because* **God has made it plain to them** *(Romans 1:18-19 NIV).*

See to it that you do not refuse him who speaks. *If they did not escape when they refused him who warned them on earth, how much less will we, if we turn away from him who warns us from heaven? At that time his voice shook the earth, but now he has promised, "Once more I will shake not only the earth but also the heavens." The words "once more" indicate the removing of what can be shaken—that is, created things—so that what cannot be shaken may remain. Therefore, since we are receiving a kingdom that cannot be shaken, let us be thankful, and so worship God acceptably* *with reverence and awe, for our **"God is a consuming fire"** (**Hebrews 12:25-29 NIV**).*

*A*ll answers for our salvation must come from Scripture and Scripture alone. There is a reason why God ordered His words to be written on parchment and not passed down from father to son by word of mouth. With time and language the story can be altered, but the written word endures forever. For this reason Shaul said even if an angel of light were to come and teach you anything other than what the Scriptures tell you, do not believe him.

> *But even if we or an angel from heaven should preach a gospel other than the one we preached to you, let them be under God's curse!* (**Galatians 1:8 NIV**)

I want to leave you with this to think about. Consider Judgment Day. Who or what will judge us in the end? By what measure will we be judged? Consider Yeshua's words:

> *But do not think I will accuse you before the Father. Your accuser is Moses [Torah], on whom your hopes are set* (***John 5:45 NIV***).

May Adonai be praised and glorified from this day on and forever. May all people know His truth and may His will be done on earth as it is in heaven.

May this book shed some light to those who read it and open a new dimension of understanding. May it influence a change and help transform you to become like Yeshua Ha'Mashiach, so you can be found righteous and holy.

Let us not fall into the fire of God; instead let us be welcomed into His kingdom for a glorious life with no end.

May the truth prevail and set us free. Amen.

HEBREW GLOSSARY

Adonai - God or Lord.
Avraham - Abraham.
Beit Lechem - Bethlehem, the house of bread.
Benyamin - Benjamin.
Chaya - Eve, also known as Chava in Hebrew.
Davar -Written word.
Derech - Way.
Galut - Diaspora (Greek for "dispersed").
Dibber - To speak or utter.
Eser Dibrot - Ten words refers to the Ten Commandments.
Isiyim- Sons of fire.
Gan Eden - Garden of Eden, garden of delight.
Pardes - Paradise.
Hanoch - Enoch.
Havel - Abel.
Ishai - Jesse.
Kodesh - Holy or separated.
Kotz - Stroke or tittle.
Ktuvim - The writings.
Mashiach - Messiah.
Matityahu - Matthew.
Moshe - Moses.
Netzer Ishai - Root of Jesse.

Nevi'im - The prophets.

Noach - Noah.

Parush - Pharisees.

Rabbi - Teacher.

Rabbinic - Legal authority, legislators.

Rachel - Rachel.

Ruach - Spirit or wind.

Shabbat - Sabbath.

Shaliach - Apostle.

Shavuot - Pentecost.

Shaul - Paul.

Shem - Son of Noah.

Shet - Seth.

Shimon - Harkening, one who listens (Simon Peter).

Shma - A central prayer or saying in the Jewish faith (taken from Deuteronomy 6:4-5).

Shmor - Guard.

Shlomo - Solomon

Tanakh - Torah, Nevi'im, Ktuvim, (Genesis to Malachi).

Torah - Pentateuch (Genesis, Exodus, Leviticus, Numbers and Deuteronomy).

Tzadaq - Made righteous.

Tzadikim - Righteous.

Tzemach - Plant, branch or shoot.

Ya'akov - Jacob or James.

Yeshua - The Hebrew word for Jesus, meaning "salvation."

Yeshayahu - Isaiah.

Yitzhak - Isaac.

Yafet - Japheth.

Yehudah - Judah.

Yerushalaim - Jerusalem.

Yochanan - John.

Yod - Jot.

Yosef - Joseph.

Yoseph Ben Matityahoo - Josephus, son of Mathaias.

CPSIA information can be obtained
at www.ICGtesting.com
Printed in the USA
LVHW101040191122
733591LV00018B/261